For further information:
e:mail niexcellence@aol.com
or call 0044 79 7628 3896

ISBN 0-9546171-2-6

IRELAND'S
EXCELLENCE

EXCELLENCE PUBLICATIONS Ltd.

Oifig an Taoisigh
Office of the Taoiseach

I am delighted to support the publication of **"Ireland's Excellence"** and welcome the opportunity provided by this publication to tell the story of an energetic and dynamic Ireland, proud of its past and confident of its future.

I am also pleased that the **Special Olympics Movement in Ireland** will benefit from the profit from sales of this book. The Games, held in 2003, catered for over 7000 athletes from 160 countries. It was the first occasion that they were held outside the United States which in itself was a real honour for Ireland.

The Games were undoubtedly an outstanding success for all involved and they are something that the whole island of Ireland can be extremely proud of. It is important to remember that the work of the **Special Olympics Movement in Ireland** continues and needs support from all quarters. **Ireland's Excellence** helps promote Ireland whilst also supporting an extremely worthwhile cause.

Bertie Ahern TD
Taoiseach

INTERNATIONAL REPUTATION.
NOW IN LOCAL OWNERSHIP.

OUR WORK

We welcome briefs from all organisations, large and small, who share the vision that *Excellence* is more *cost-effective* than *Mediocrity*.

LyleBailie
INTERNATIONAL

SPECIALISTS IN ATTITUDE & BEHAVIOUR CHANGE

31 Bruce Street, Belfast BT2 7JD **T** 028 9033 1044 **F** 028 9033 1272 **E** directors@lylebailie.com www.lylebailie.com

FOREWORD

The idea behind publishing Ireland's Excellence came from the publication of its sister volume, **Excellence – Northern Ireland.** Accordingly, the idea emerged to bring together a volume portraying all that is excellent about Ireland. It is, of course, impossible to include everything and everyone who has made an excellent contribution to our island; indeed we have tried to highlight many less well-known examples. Some of the scenes, the people and the achievements will be familiar to you, others less so, but altogether we hope you agree that Ireland is a truly special place and one of which we are extremely proud.

We hope that this book will help promote Ireland at home and abroad. Profits from the sales of the book will go to the Irish Special Olympics Movement to help build on the fantastic work that was done in 2003 before, during and after the Irish Special Olympics 2003 - an event that we can all be particularly proud of.

This book could not have been produced without a huge amount of work and support from many quarters. To all those who contributed in whatever way, we are truly grateful.

We hope you will support Ireland, and the Irish Special Olympics Movement, by purchasing a copy.

Excellence Publications Ltd

I R E L A N D ' S
EXCELLENCE
CONTENTS

IRELAND'S
EXCELLENT FACTS

A collection of some of the lesser known snippets of interest from all over Ireland.

Excellent Facts

Things you never knew about Ireland

The Irish certainly know how to tell a tale or two. From the epic legend of Cuchulain to stories of banshees, wizards and even little people, Irish history is steeped in myths and folklore.

The Greek astronomer and geographer Ptolemy believed it to be a land permanently covered by fog and inhabited by man-eating giants. In the 12th century, the Norman-Welsh chronicler Giraldus Cambrensis wrote of a country with islands where people could live forever and on which no woman could set foot and live. In 1572, the Englishman Edmund Campion, sent as a spy by Elizabeth I, returned from Ireland with a report full of so many oddities that it ultimately cost him his head.

Romantic as these tales may be, Ireland is also a country rich with excellent facts. It's a land that has given birth to literary brilliance, inspired visions of vampires and seen villages buried by sandstorms. In other words, real stories worth telling.

Strange truths

It has been said that windmills always turn counter clockwise – except for the windmills in Ireland. Blennerville Windmill is Ireland's only commercially operated windmill. It is also the tallest of its kind in Europe: 21.3 metres high.

In 1853 in Enagh Monmore, Ireland, a bog about a mile in circumference started flowing downhill and continued until it was stopped by a rise in the ground's contour a day later.

On the 13th anniversary of the Munich air disaster, which wiped out the famous 'Busby Babes' football team, Manchester United played Coventry. The only goal of the game was scored by United's new Irish signing Liam O'Brien at 3.04pm – the exact moment of impact three decades before.

James Byrne, the 7 feet 2 inch 'Irish Giant', died of depression in 1783 after being literally watched to death by the servant of a doctor who wanted his huge frame for dissection.

A monkey appears on the Fitzgerald coat of arms in tribute to the family pet, which rescued the infant First Earl of Kildare from a fire at Kilkea castle in the 14th century.

The crypt of St. Michan's Church in Dublin contains the almost perfectly preserved remains of corpses dating from the Middle Ages. The reason for their incorruption appears to be the limestone walls of their tombs.

The Busby Babes
Football Team
(left)

Fitzgerald Coat of Arms
(top)

Blennerville Windmill
(opposite)

Squire Watson, an eccentric 18th century Kilkenny landowner had such an unshakeable belief that he would be reincarnated as a fox that he had a luxurious marble den built in the grounds of his estate in anticipation of his return.

Until the 1920s, on St. Brigid's Day at Teltown, County Meath, couples could legally marry by simply walking towards each other. Should the marriage not work out, they could divorce by walking away from each other at the same place exactly a year later.

Dermot MacMurrough, who was responsible for bringing the Normans into Ireland, rotted to death for his sin in 1173, after contracting morbis pediculosis.

During a night in 1986, a 600-yard stretch of peat bog engulfed a road between Ballycastle and Belderg in Ireland's County Mayo, taking with it a small forest of three-foot pine saplings. The bog was three or four feet deep, and covered the road, which was 18 feet wide.

The famous Irish general Owen Roe O'Neill, who never received so much as a scratch during a military career spanning 30 years, died of blood poisoning after stepping on a rusty nail in 1649.

In 1895, Irishman James Harden Hickey wrote a bestseller entitled *The Aesthetics of Suicide* listing 139 ways of ending one's life. Three years later he killed himself!

In 1770, the entire village of Rosapenna on Donegal's Inishowen Peninsula was buried overnight by a freak sandstorm.

The lunar-like landscape of the Burren in County Clare is the only place in the world where artic and sub-tropical flora grow side by side.

Oxmantown in Dublin, part of the site of the old Viking city, has the highest concentration of blondes in Ireland.

Who would have thought?

Dublin born Bram Stoker, who lived in Marino Crescent, Clontarf and attended Trinity College Dublin, introduced the character of Count Dracula of Transylvania in his classic horror novel *Dracula* (1897).

Mary Robinson was elected to office in 1990 - a milestone event in Irish society. Not only was she the first woman president of Ireland she was, at the time, one of only three female heads of state in the world.

MGM's roaring lion was bred in Dublin Zoo.

John Robert Gregg
14th August 1942 receiving a honourary Degree of Doctrine of letters
(top)

Mary Robinson
(bottom left)

The Burren in Co. Clare
(opposite)

John Robert Gregg, born on June 17th 1867 in Shantonagh, Derryvalley, in Ballybay, Co Monaghan, was an inventor who developed the shorthand system.

Irish chemist and natural philosopher, Robert Boyle (born 1627), from Lismore County Waterford was a founding member of the Royal Society of London. He formulated the law of physics that bears his name: Boyles law.

Sir William Rowan Hamilton, born Dublin 1805, was a mathematician and astronomer who developed the theory of quaternions, a landmark in the development of algebra, and discovered the phenomenon of conical refraction.

William Parsons, Third Earl of Rosse (1800-1867) built a huge telescope in Birr, County Offaly, in 1845 and discovered the shape of new galaxies. It was the largest telescope in the world from 1845 until well into the 20th century.

Dublin housewife Kit Welsh disguised herself as a man and served 20 years in the army of the Duke of Marlborough from 1692. She was wounded four times without doctors discovering her secret, and survived to be personally decorated for bravery by Queen Anne.

Turkish Delight chocolate was first made in Cobh, County Cork, by the Hadji Bey company in the 20th century.

On average 1,000,000 pints of Guinness are consumed every day in Ireland.

On average 10,000,000 glasses of Guinness are consumed worldwide.

Downing Street in London is named after the 17th century Dublin-born politician, Sir Charles Downing.

Kilkenny born James Hobbon was the architect, designer and builder of The White House.

Robert Boyle
(top left)

Rowan Hamilton
(middle)

William Parsons
(bottom)

The White House
(top right)

The Oscar statuette was designed by a Dublin-born art director Cedric Gibbons. He went on to win nine.

ESB International, a leading international power and engineering company, has operations in over 40 countries from the UK to Indonesia, through Europe, the Middle East, Asia and Africa. ESBI has completed contracts in more than 100 countries over the past twenty-five years.

In 2002 The Shannon Scheme, Ardnacrusha hydroelectric station was awarded the International Milestone and International Landmark awards, joining the Eiffel Tower and Golden Gate Bridge in engineering excellence.

In 2004 ESB has in excess of 9000 megawatts of power under its control in Ireland and abroad.

Most of the *Book of Kells* was actually written in a monastery of Iona.

Arguably the oddest criminal in history was 'Billy the Bowl', who terrorised the streets of 18th century Dublin. Born without legs, Billy moved around in an iron bowl specially made for him by a sympathetic blacksmith. Tiring of begging for a living, Billy turned to robbery and murder before his arrest and execution in 1786.

**The Shannon Scheme
Ardnacrusha Hydro Electric
Station Co. Clare**
(top)

Statue of St. Patrick
(above)

Book of Kells
(bottom)

Success at home

and abroad.

In 1927, we brought electricity to Ireland for the first time.
Today, we are a leading international power and engineering company,
with operations in over 40 countries around the world.

What a place!

Dublin is the only city in the world to have produced three Nobel prizewinners for literature: W.B. Yeats (1923), George Bernard Shaw (1925) and Samuel Beckett (1969).

Ireland's holiest place is arguably the churchyard of St. Eanna on the Aran Island of Inis Mor. Over 120 recognised saints are buried there.

The world's most northerly vineyard is in Mallow, County Cork.

The only nudist beach in Ireland is at the Forty Foot Leap, by the Sandycove Martello tower, in Dun Laoghaire.

Since it opened in 1830, Dublin's Clasnevin Cemetery has been the resting place for more than 11 million people.

Phoenix Park in Dublin covers 1800 acres. It is the largest city park in the world.

Europe's highest cliffs are on Achill Island, off County Mayo. Dropping over 2000 feet into the Atlantic Ocean, they are nearly twice the height of the world's tallest building.

The prehistoric tomb at Newgrange in County Meath is older than the Great Pyramids of Egypt.

Emmet Square in Birr, County Offaly, marks the centre of Ireland.

Samuel Beckett
(top right)

Aran Memorials
(middle)

Achill Island
(bottom left)

*Newgrange Megalithic
passage tomb in
County Meath*

Horse racing in Ireland

Ireland is the third largest producer of thoroughbreds worldwide with some 10,500 foals annually.

Ireland accounts for in excess of 42% of total output of thoroughbreds in the EU.

Bloodstock breeding is the fastest growing sector of Irish Livestock over the past five years

The top stallions in the world are generally recognised as coming from Ireland.

Horse racing, breeding and betting industries account for some 13,000 people in full-time employment. 25,000 people earn an income from the horse racing industry equating to approximately 1.5% of the Irish workforce.

1.4 million people attended race meetings in Ireland last year.

Race meeting account for 50,000 overseas tourist visitors per annum.

The total value of assets employed by the industry is 2.5 billion euro.

Irish racing is the highest quality racing in the world and boasts the highest prize money in Europe.

364 overseas owners have invested here and there are over 6,000 active owners involved in the business.

Hardy Eustace
jumping a hurdle on way to victory in the Champion hurdle at Cheltenhem 2004
(above)

Monty's Pass
winning the Grand National at Aintree 2003
(right)

Our *people* make us what we are...

...the most comprehensive and professional publishing solution in Ireland.

A publishing solution from TSO Ireland delivers unique added value benefits to our customers.

The information path incorporates data capture, appropriate design, quality print, multiple publishing options, storage, distribution and access to a retail, wholesale and online sales network.

The best bit?
All this is available through a single point of contact.

You may not need all our services right away but our flexible solutions mean you can choose the options you want.

It's simple really - we'll help you keep it that way.

The Information Management Company

For further information call
028 9023 8451
email enquiries@tsoireland.com
or visit www.tsoireland.com

IRELAND'S
PRIDE OF PLACE

An insight into how some of the places in Ireland have derived their name.

Pride of Place
The naming of Ireland

Studying a map of Ireland can tell you more than just the routes to take. An understanding of Irish place names and how they have been translated into English can let you read into the history of the country and enable you to learn about the topography.

Many of the place names in Ireland are anglicised versions of the way the original Irish (Gaelic) name was spoken. The settlers tried to preserve the place names by writing them phonetically in English. Although this resulted in some beautiful sounding place names, it lost the meaning behind them.

The layout of the land is divided into four provinces consisting of 32 counties. These in turn are divided into parishes and townlands, of which there are over 60,000. To try to name or study them all would be almost impossible!

The importance of place names is significant, as they reflect the various layers of settlement that have made Ireland into the country it is today. Often they have been influenced by geographical features such as trees, rivers, loughs and types of land within a settlement, or in some cases even animals and parts of the human body. Ireland's numerous loughs and rivers are reflected in many place names but through anglicisation of the Gaelic they have been somewhat altered. A prime 'example of this is 'Abhainn', the Irish word for river, which has lent itself to 'Awbeg' (Abha Bheag) in Co. Cork and Limerick and 'Bunowen' (Bun na hAbhann) in Co. Mayo. Native trees are also well represented eg. 'Ballynure' in Co.Donegal translated from the Gaelic 'baile an lúir' – 'Iúr being the Irish word for yew.

It's no surprise, in a land famous for its saints, that many place names have their origins in spiritual figures and buildings. It can usually be assumed that places containing the names of Patrick and Brigid, such as Downpatrick, Croagh Patrick and Kilbreedy, refer to the Saint Patrick and Saint Brigid who are two of Ireland's best known saints. However, to identify a particular saint in a place

St Patrick at Saul, Downpatrick
(opposite)

Croagh Patrick Mountain
(left)

name can be difficult to distinguish, as there have been many with the same name resident in Ireland through the course of its history. Place names abound with words such as cill, dun, rath and lios, reflecting many different types of religious and military settlements. In the other half of the place name, a descriptive word or a topographical feature is normally found. For example, one of the most important events in St. Brigid's life was the foundation of Kildare Cathedral. The cathedral started out as a small 'kill' or church, built near a great oak tree. It was from the church and tree that the surrounding area took its name ***Cill-Dara 'church of the oak'*** or ***'church near the oak'***. This later extended to the town, county and finally diocese.

Naturally, the coming of Christianity brought many Latin borrowings, which have also been altered in translation. There are at least three dozen place names beginning with 'Donagh', derived from the Latin word 'Domhnach' and meaning the Lord's Day.

Predominantly, place names are Irish. Lann, a very old Irish word, seems to have meant simply 'place' and later was used to denote 'church'. It can be found in many place names throughout the country.

The arrival of the Vikings in 897 AD left its mark in a small number of Norse influenced names including *'Wicklow'* meaning *'meadow of the bay'* and *'Carlingford'* meaning *'rough or rapid fjord'*.

In the 17th century, the plantation of Scottish settlers brought elements such as 'burn' and 'brae' into the dictionary of place names. However, the most significant influence on Irish names came from English, which is evident in the Irish capital. ***The official name of the city is 'Baile Átha Cliath', which means town of the hurdle ford*** but as the postmark on any letter will show, the more widely known and used name is 'Dublin. Most naming is now done in English although Irish names in anglicised form often reappear.

Dunamase Fort
Co. Laois
(opposite)

Ha'penny Bridge
Dublin
(above)

Naturally, the political and cultural divide in the country has had a significant impact on how certain place names are referred to. After the foundation of the Irish Free State in 1922, some names were changed including *Kingstown in Co. Dublin*, which became *Dún Laoghaire* (pronounced 'Dunleary' by English speakers and 'Doonlairah' by Irish speakers) and *Queenstown in Co. Cork* reverted to *Cobh* (pronounced 'cove'). *King's County* and *Queen's County* were renamed *Co. Laois* and *Co. Offaly* in 1921.

However the complex relationship between the English and Irish really began in 1829 when the Ordnance Survey was introduced and surveyors wrote Irish names with English spelling. The most common changes included the aspiration of letters such as bh and mh, which both sound like v or w, hence the re-naming of 'Ardbhaile' in Co. Donegal to 'Ardvalley'.

Birr Castle
Co. Offaly
(below)

THE DRIVE TO
SAVE LIVES

NEVER EVER DRINK & DRIVE

National Safety Council

NO SEATBELT NO EXCUSE

National Safety Council

slow
down
boys

National Safety Council

PAY ATTENTION
OR PAY THE PRICE

National Safety Council

PAY ATTENTION
OR PAY THE PRICE

National Safety Council

GET THE POINT
NOT THE POINTS!

National Safety Council

National Safety Council

National Safety Council, 4 Northbrook Road, Banelagh, Dublin, IRELAND.
T: 003531 496 3422 W: www.nsc.ie

The capital city Dublin was where the Norsemen moored their longboats. The Irish thought of the river more as a barrier and named it after their way of getting across: Bailie Atha Cliath, the town of the hurdle ford.

Dublin View

IRELAND'S
HISTORY AND HERITAGE

Foras na Gaeilge

AN CHUAIRD DEISIL
A journey in Irish culture

T he high kings of Ireland showed their domination of the whole country by travelling the circuit of the island. This showed their power clearly, increased their knowledge of their people and their awareness of different conditions in different parts of the land. It was a unifying factor, and the capacity to complete the circuit was one of the tests of real high kingship. The journey began and ended at the king's capital – often Tara – and invariably followed the same pattern, heading south, then west, then north. This journey, following the right hand and the course of the sun, was called 'an chuaird deisil', the circuit of the right hand. Here we follow a chuaird designed to show just some of the evidence of the continuing excellence of Irish culture in Ireland. The choice of route and the selection and description of the evidence is as subjective as any king's must have been – or as any bard's.

Dublin

Dublin, Dubhlinn or the black pool was where Norsemen moored their longboats. The Irish thought of the river more as a barrier, and named it after their way of getting across: Baile Átha Cliath, the town of the hurdle ford. Dublin has been bilingual or trilingual ever since. Its writers include Mairtín Ó Cadhain, who knew the city's layout particularly well, for political reasons, and Mairtín Ó Direáin, registrar of the National Gallery, whose mature poetry about the city may last longer than his nostalgia for his native Arran Islands. The living poet, Nuala Ní Dhomhnaill has gained an international following not because of a rural setting but because the sophistication of her poetry is underpinned by research in the Folklore Archive in University College. They are as much Dublin writers as are Wilde, Synge, Joyce, Beckett and Eavan Boland.

At the same time as Swift lived and wrote in Dublin, and about the time Goldsmith was attending Trinity College, the leading figures in Dublin Irish language circles were the poet-scholar father

Viking ship
at Kildare Place
(above)

Reconstruction of Dublin
c.1000 A.D.
(opposite)

Clomacnoise
Co. Offlay
(below)

and son Seán and Tadhg Ó Neachtain. Backing the Jacobites when that was no longer profitable, and given to the manic punning later seen as typical of Irish letters, they show that obsession with the past, the 'backward look' which Frank O'Connor said was a mark of the Irish mind -but also an anarchic sense of humour, a bleak sense of reality, and a rebellious iconoclasm.

Handel's *Messiah* was first performed in 1742 in the Music Hall in Fishamble Street, Sráid Sheamlas an Éisc. This part of Dublin still resounds with the choirs and the carillons of Christ Church and St Patrick's cathedrals. In Handel's time, and for some time afterwards, Irish was the common vernacular of Dublin and, as has been shown by A J Bliss and others, much affected the works in English of Dean Swift. 'Gulliver' could be a command to a large servant- A Ghiolla Mhóir. In music, the Gaelic style held its own. There was a celebrated musical duel between Carolan, composer and harper, and Geminiani, composer and violinist, which ended when Geminiani played a concerto by Vivaldi and Carolan was then able to play the same, which he had never heard before, note perfect. He went on to compose and play, on the spot, his own concerto along the lines of Vivaldi's - *Carolan's Concerto*.

The *Book of Durrow* is a small manuscript named after the monastery of Durrow, a foundation of Colm Cille near Tullamore in central Ireland. It was kept in this place from the 7th century until the 17th century. The manuscript is now held in Trinity College Dublin. The *Book of Durrow* shows development from the even earlier 6th century *Cathach of St Colm Cille*, which is now in the Royal Irish Academy. The 8th century *Book of Kells*, now in Trinity College Dublin, is the most richly ornate earlier Irish manuscript. All of these were in Latin but the earliest manuscript in Irish is the late 11th century *Leabhar na hUidhre*, the *Book of the Dun Cow*, probably written at Clonmacnoise. It was named after St Ciaran's pet cow whose hide was

preserved as a relic and may have been used to bind the sacred manuscript.

Clonmacnoise

Clonmacnoise is one of the most peaceful places in Ireland. It is a large monastic site with the wide Shannon beside it, a site with no evidence of modernity obtruding. But it was not always peaceful. The monastery itself was raided and eventually destroyed. The wars of Ireland have given us comparatively few prose texts in Irish. But one letter survives from 1600, to an Irish notable from near Clonmacnoise who was slow to join in the Nine Years War. Friar Clyn of Kilkenny wrote his annals of the Black Death, the great plague of 1349. He died of the plague himself, concluding his account: "for fear of these annals remaining unfinished, I leave behind some paper hoping that some one of Adam's sons will survive this plague and will finish this work." Up to one half of the population of the Pale and English areas died. Mortality in the Gaelic areas, less densely populated, was less. This, coming soon after the Bruce invasion was too much, and the AngloNorman colony lost strength and retreated for two hundred years. Many areas of settlement, even close to the Pale, became Irish speaking. The Statutes of Kilkenny 1366 attempted to legislate for the situation and banned elements of Irish dress, fashion, speech, games -all the elements of Gaelic civilisation.

Clonmacnoise Crozier
Clonmacnoise, Co. Offaly
11th century
(above)

" Now many of the English of the said land, forsaking the English language, fashion, mode of riding, laws and usages, live and govern themselves according to the manners, fashion and languages of the Irish enemies and also have made divers marriages and alliances between themselves and the Irish enemies aforesaid; whereby the said land and the liege people thereof, the English language, the allegiance due to our lord the King and the English laws are put in subjection and decayed and the Irish enemies exalted and raised up contrary to right."

Rock of Cashel
Hore Abbey
(below)

Cashel

Cashel of the Kings is a limestone crop rising high above the rich valley of the Suir. Its remarkable silhouette reflects the needs of power and worship, of kings and archbishops. Brian Boru centred his kingship here, before going on to become high king and finally defeating the Vikings in 1014. A complex of buildings includes a fine round tower and the pre-Norman Cormac's Chapel, one of the first and best examples of the Romanesque style fusing native and continental elements of architecture and decoration. The site shows the harshness of history but also the indomitable survival of the past. From Cashel, a path follows the bank of the Suir river southwards. No tarmac road comes near, and the only noise is of water moving in weirs and of swans' wings beating the air. Peace comes dropping slow and water, lush

vegetation, cattle and many ruined buildings (mills, abbeys, fortified houses) give a sense of continuity.

Travelling the cuaird deisil the observer will see that people in different places lived in different ways at different times. The Pale, the areas earliest and most continually settled from Britain, saw a three-field system and stone-lined elaborate ditching. In most of the rest of Ireland, the economy was based on cattle rather than on crops, hedging and ditching was simple, and the practice of transhumance, or moving flocks to higher pasture in the summer continued. Buaile was the summer bothy and dairying place, where the young enjoyed greater freedom. The rural economy meant that villages did not grow except in that area of the Pale, or later under the influence of landlords. The population on the land was in individual dwellings or smaller clusters often called clochán or baile, where there was a degree of close co-operation in the major shared tasks of the year, the meitheal. This tradition of individual dwelling places remains a personal preference for many and therefore a planning issue. The Irish had developed urban living patterns near the great monasteries, themselves considerable centres of educational, artistic, craft and trading activity, and also episcopal centres such as Rosacarbery, but history did not allow them to develop.

Carrick on Suir

Moving now to Carrick on Suir, the place where Anne Boleyn may have been from. She could well have been the reason why Shakespeare had one of his characters, Pistol in Henry V, sing "Calen o cusure me", cailín ó chois tSiúre mé - I'm a girl from the banks of the Suir. Her daughter, Elizabeth I, established Trinity College, Dublin, and took a keen interest in the furtherance of the reformation of Ireland by the provision of teaching and texts in the Irish language.

North Mall and Shandon Steeple
Cork City
(below)

Cork

The second city in the Republic, Cork relates to the water in the same way, they say, as does Venice. The complexity of its bridge system confuses and delights the stranger. Cork is a major literary centre, with an important jazz festival and a significant film festival. It plays internationally, and has always done so. One of the pieces of Shostakovich most often played, his romance from the film music of *The Gadfly*, was based on a novel by Cork woman E L Voynich née Boole. Seán Ó Riada, a lecturer at Cork University who lived at the nearby Gaeltacht area of Cúil Aodha, developed Irish traditional music into the sophisticated artform it has become, bringing it into close contact with European music and insisting on its standards.

The Blasket Islands off the southwest coast,

evacuated in the 1950s, held a small community, from which was written some of the best prose of the 20th century in Irish. Maxim Gorki's autobiographical writings showed Tomás Ó Criomhthainn that a record of an ordinary life, plainly told, could have value. He, Peig Sayers and Muiris Ó Súilleabháin created a shelf of books 'ná beidh a leithéid arís ann' - the likes of which will not occur again. The atmosphere of the island was such that newcomers fell under its influence immediately.

Limerick and Galway

The main towns of Ireland are and were port towns around the coast. Although the countryside was relatively poor, these towns traded successfully with Britain and the continent of Europe, and much of the wealth of Ireland was concentrated in them. Luke Gernon visited Limerick in 1620 and he noted that the inner city, the part situated on the island, was well built and contained many good houses. The town is "a lofty building of marble - in the High Street it is built from one gate to the other in the one form, like the colleges of Oxford, so magnificent that at my first entrance it did amaze me." It was strongly fortified, 'fenced with a huge string wall that travellers affirm they have not seen the like of in Europe.' Limerick and other ports imported wine and salt; they exported hides, linens, and coarser woollen cloths; there was also a considerable trade in fish. The merchants tended to trade in English or other countries' ships and did not develop a merchant fleet.

In 1831 John Scott Vandaleur made an agreement with his tenants at Ralahine, County Clare and they set up a co-operative, a major and revolutionary experiment in joint farming and co-operative methods which was quite successful until the landlord's gaming debts forced him to go back on the agreement.

Westward from Galway, along the broken coastline, among les lacs du Connémara there is a mixture of the very traditional and the ultramodern. This is the strongest Gaeltacht in the country, a centre of the ornate a capella singing called sean-nós. Practitioners have included Máire Áine Ní Dhonncha and the great Joe Heaney, whose international eminence was

Blasket Islands
Southwest Coast Islands
(above)

recognised with a position in the University of Seattle. Nowadays Connamara has evolved its communications in a new way. The national radio station, Raidió na Gaeltachta, the national television station, TG4, and the national weekly newspaper *Foinse* are all headquartered here, as are various satellite film companies, subtitling services, independent scriptwriters etc. Exporting abroad, and importing product from abroad, and with close links to other, particularly Celtic countries, these industries have created a new image for Ireland, and have gathered together in one place a critical mass of talented young people. This in turn has impacted on the Irish language in Galway City, on the native speaker as well as the learner. Associated with National University, Galway, an intensive language teaching centre, Áras Uí Chadhain in an Cheathrú Rua also uses sophisticated modern technology to achieve its aims of teaching communicative competence.

The main result of these innovative industries has been to service the new pride and confidence of the Irish speaker throughout the country, and indeed abroad, to facilitate a new generation and its younger style.

The Aran Islands

The Aran Islands at the mouth of Galway Bay were the birthplace of Liam O'Flaherty, a major short story writer in English and Irish, of Mairtín Ó Direáin, one of the noted poets of the 20th century in Irish, and of Breandán Ó hEithir, journalist and prosewriter, whose work in Irish provided a jolt of modernity where it was needed. The semi-circular stone fort, Dún Aengus, which uses the seacliffs as the outer half of its perimeter, attracts many visitors and may be a symbol of the language - always reported to be near the cliff-edge, but always holding on.

Connemara
Ireland
(above)

Traditional Homestead
Aran Islands
(right)

Foras na Gaeilge

Douglas Hyde from Frenchpark, Co. Roscommon spoke at a meeting of the National Literary Society, the brainchild of W.B Yeats. Hyde talked of the necessity for de-anglicising Ireland by reviving the language:

"What the battle-axe of the Dane, the sword of the Norman, the wile of the Saxon were unable to perform we have accomplished ourselves. We have at last broken the continuity of Irish life…"

The foundation of Conradh na Gaeilge followed. As a young man, the son of the manse, Hyde had learned Irish from his neighbours and wrote his diary in the language as soon as he was able.

County Mayo

Co. Mayo, praised by Camden, was beloved by Antoine O Raifterí whose desire to go home there became greater on St Brigid's Day, 1 February, the traditional start of spring. Love of the native place was very marked, and made emigration much harder. An earlier song of the misery of removal from the native place was 'Conndae Mhuigh Eo', with its first line being 'Ar an luing seo Phádraig Luingsigh'. Here I am on Patrick Lynch's ship, was translated by two young men attending an Irish class in Belfast and taught by one Patrick Lynch, who himself had collected songs in Mayo in the period immediately after 1798. One of his two young pupils in Belfast, George Fox, emigrated to make his fortune and went missing in Guyana. The other, Samuel Ferguson, became president of the Royal Irish Academy and was knighted for services to literature. He became a poet of eminence and translated widely from the Irish, creating a body of work and a poetic register which set the scene for the later Irish Revival.

William Butler Yeats, Nobel Laureate for poetry, was a member of the committee which designed the coinage of the Irish Free State. They produced a coinage which was celebrated for its beauty and practicality until recently and represented the aesthetic of the traditions of Ireland and the facts of her economy. Yeats, at one remove from the Gaelic tradition, was continually enriched by his own imaginative closeness to that tradition and liberated by the absence of the responsibilities which could come of being a part of it.

Donegal

The most northerly county in Ireland, Donegal, is famed for rugged scenery and a spectacular coastline. It may have been that environment which gave rise to those who created its other claim to fame - writers. Ciaran Carson's comment: "I wonder if the disciplined wilderness of Donegal music has anything to do with this terrain", could well apply to the writing as well as to the music. With an imagination formed by the elements, a linguistic gift honed by bilingualism, a bedrock of tradition and much experience of seasonal and long-term emigration, the Donegal writers in both Irish and English have been of major importance throughout the 20th century. Examples of older writers include Séamus MacManus, Patrick McGill and Peadar O'Donnell, and more recently, Frank McGuinness and Moya Cannon. Writers and artists such as Jennifer Johnson, Brian Friel and the artists Paul Henry and Derek Hill often come to Donegal for inspiration . The county is aware that its continuing Gaelic heritage is an asset, and has developed cultural tourism with classes in language and culture in places such as the archaeologically rich Glencolmcille of Oideas

Cael, the Frankie Kennedy Winter School of Music under Errigal mountain and the Tory Island weekends of culture and craic.

Derry and Antrim

Counties Derry and Antrim, the counties which show the closest relationship to Scotland down the centuries, retain many elements of both Scottish and Gaelic Irish culture. Traditional Irish flute playing mixes with the marching band tradition. Ballad singers like David Hammond, and players like Derek Bell, immerse themselves in and extend the two traditions within one. John Hewitt, poet and regionalist, was the precursor to a diffuse group of poets – Seamus Heaney, Derek Mahon, James Simmons, Michael Longley, Seamus Deane – who acknowledged his importance, and were liberated by it.

Belfast

Belfast is a city of contrasts, of lines drawn as engineering blueprints or as poetry, as barriers or for musical scores. Major investment in the cultural institutions of Northern Ireland started in the 1960s. But culture is what occurs, naturally, and so Ulster has its own traits and characteristics. Some of these are shared with Scotland, such as the negative Cha in Irish – elsewhere ní - and the prevalence of dialect words such as thonder in English or Ulster-Scots. Other aspects are man made and reflect the province's past, such as Carrickfergus Castle, a magnificent Norman castle in a very good state of repair. The Linen Hall Library in Belfast is evidence for the liberal spirit

Carrickfergus Castle
Carrickfergus, Co. Antrim
(above)

Hands Across the Divide
Derry City
(right)

of enquiry dominant in east Ulster at the time of its foundation, the 1790s, while the Ulster Museum, the Ulster Folk and Transport Museum and the Public Record Office show the confidence of curators facing the past with an open awareness, considerable resources and a high level of exhibition skills. The Belfast Harpers Festival held around 12 July 1792 was intended to rescue the remnants of a great tradition. The festival has succeeded, and the harping tradition survives today in the Ulster Harpers' Orchestra.

An equally courageous musical initiative, not in Belfast but at the foot of Strangford Lough, is the fashionable Castle Ward Opera, a company which chose a barn as venue for first rate opera.   The experience is magic. Castle Ward itself is a building with two faces, one classical and the other Gothic. Bernard Ward, the first Lord Bangor and his wife Lady Anne had two very different ideas of what they wanted and made no effort to compromise. Even the interior decoration of the rooms shows this division of taste. The area has been the setting for bleaker writing, such as Sam Hanna Bell's *December Bride*, the short fiction of Michael McLaverty and for lighter music such as Percy French's *Mountains of Mourne*.

Music and writing are as much a part of Ulster's past and present as of anywhere else in Ireland. Medbh McGuckian, Ciaran Carson and Paul Muldoon are in the first rank of poets, while musicians have included the popular Jimmy Kennedy and Van Morrison. The heritage of music and song has been maintained by singers and teachers such as Pádraigín Ní Uallacháin and Jerry Hicks and in schools and festivals in places like Tí Chulainn, near Mullaghbawn (an Mullach Bán, the white summit).

Linen Hall Library
Belfast
(below)

The position of the Irish language in the community is a complex one. Poster advertising may sometimes used imaginatively the levels of bilingualism which exist, as in a St Patrick's Day period campaign by 'Cadbury's, the Irish for Chocolate,' with the image of chocolate marked seacláid. Street signs, directional signs and bus scrolls all reflect the sense of place and its connection with the language which makes sense of many of the place names. The highest offices of state are given Irish titles on all occasions (Taoiseach, Tánaiste, Ceann Comhairle, Teachta Dála) and the places relating to them may be named only in Irish (Áras an Uachtaráin, Dáil Éireann). Major official corporate bodies often have their titles recognised in universal or near-universal usage in Irish -Garda, Aer Lingus - or in initials, RTÉ, C.I.E. Other names are commonly but not exclusively used: Roinn an Taoisigh, an Slua Muirí.

IRELAND'S
PEOPLE & ACHIEVEMENTS

Writers, explorers, scientists, artists and world statesmen - all from Ireland

Louis le Brocquy
The Art of Excellence

How did a painter with no formal training become a dominant force in Irish art for over six decades? The story begins in Dublin, 1916. While Patrick Pearse and the Irish Citizen Army were painting the town red in the bloody Easter Rising, one of Ireland's most celebrated artists was born to Irish parents of Belgian decent. As a child, Louis le Brocquy did not recognise his talent. Nor did he show much interest. Remarking on his youth, Louis, in his own words, is said to have "regarded painting as nothing more or less than a diversion" and without protest drifted through chemistry classes into his grandfather's Dublin oil refinery.

However, during this time, paintings that he had been familiar with in reproduction, those of Rembrandt, Goya and Manet, amongst others, suddenly started to enthrall the young industrial chemist, leading him to abandon the family ship and set sail for Europe to study the great masters. In strange cities and "alone with the great artists of the past" he became vividly aware, for the first time, of his Irish identity to which he has remained attached all his life.

With no formal training, Louis studied by himself at the National Gallery, London, the Louvre, Paris, in Venice and Geneva, then the temporary home of the Prado during the Spanish Civil War. He was enthralled by Spanish painting, its use of grey and white remaining constantly important in his work. Returning through France to Ireland in 1940, the controversial rejection of his paintings by the RHA signaled the advent of the Irish Exhibition of Living Art of which le Brocquy was a founding member. In 1946 le Brocquy moved to London where he worked for a decade and became well known as a younger member of a contemporary group, which included artists such as Nicholson, Sutherland, Scott and Bacon, with whom the British Council exhibited his work internationally.

Initially, le Brocquy's developing art underwent a series of radical changes. His early works (1939-45), including *Girl in White*, (Ulster Museum, Belfast) established his ongoing preoccupation with the individual. The Tinker paintings of the late 1940s such as *Tinkers Resting* (Tate Gallery, London) developed early concerns relating to human isolation and outcasts. The Grey Period (1950-1956), including *A Family* (National Gallery of Ireland), contemplated a stark human circumstance in the aftermath of the Second World War.

In 1955, *Ambassador Magazine* commissioned le Brocquy to tour Spain and to create textile designs for British printed and woven fabrics. Once again he was deeply impressed by what an exciting, infinitely varied country Spain was, but this particular visit gave him what he said was "an entirely new perception of the meaning of light". That year he painted *Figures in Sunlight*, leading to the Presence Series, 1956-64.

In 1956 le Brocquy represented Ireland at the Venice Biennale where his painting, *A Family*, was awarded the Premio Acquisto Internationale. In 1958 *A Family*, was included in the historic exhibition 'Fifty Years of Modern Art at the Brussels World Fair' and, in the same year, he married the young Irish painter, Anne Madden, leaving London to work with her in the comparative isolation of the French Midi.

According to *A Painter Seeing His Way*, his wife's account of his life, le Brocquy destroyed much of his work in 1963. Then a visit, in 1964, to the Musee de l'Homme in Paris, proved both seminal and catalytic. His discovery there of the Polynesian Ancestral Head, "the magic box that contains the spirit", motivated a long series of head images.

Louis le Brocquy
(opposite)

This preoccupation with painting heads, usually emerging from a white ground, became the core focus of his work, leading to the Head Series (1964-1996) including *Head of an Irish Martyr* (Hirshhorn Museum and Sculpture Garden, Washington DC) which rekindled his interest in the Celtic head culture. Initially anonymous, these images later depicted Irish literary figures such as Joyce, Yeats, Beckett and Heaney.

Since 1996, le Brocquy has embarked on a body of works entitled *Human Images* and designed a unique series of tapestries, woven in Aubusson, France, including his immense series of twenty five Táin Tapestries (Irish Museum of Modern Art). Those from the 1950s, notably *Adam and Eve in the Garden* (Hugh Lane Gallery of Modern Art, Dublin), are graphically based on contemporary paintings. His illustrations have graced such classic books as James Joyce's *Dubliners* and Samuel Beckett's *Stirring Still* and he designed the set and costumes for *Waiting for Godot* at the Gate Theatre, Dublin and the Lincoln Centre, New York.

Le Brocquy's work has been honoured with museum retrospectives in Ireland, France, Japan, Belgium, Australia and the USA and represented in numerous collections worldwide. He is also the first and only living artist ever to be included in the Irish Collection of the National Gallery of Ireland.

The inner nature of le Brocquy's work is perhaps best understood by turning to his own experience:

"I suppose initially I simply wanted to become a good painter, to join in the spiritual excitement of a great creative tradition. But finally I have come to think that painting- the act of painting- has somehow enabled me to reach towards, even to touch something of our inner human reality."

Isolated Being. 1962,
Hugh Lane Municipal Gallery
(left)

The Art of Graceful Living.

The Merrion is unique.

Behind the refined exterior of four lovingly restored Georgian townhouses, Dublin's most luxurious
5 star hotel has revived a 200 year old tradition of gracious living amidst elegant surroundings.

At The Merrion, the spirit of hospitality is as unquenchable as it was when Lord Monck entertained in
these great rooms two centuries ago. Expect a welcome as warm as its roaring log fires. And attentive service
as detailed as the exquisite Rococo plasterwork above you.

A stay here redefines relaxation with the shimmering infinity pool and state-of-the-art gym as well
as the treatment rooms of The Tethra Spa. And as home to the renowned Restaurant Patrick Guilbaud,
overlooking authentic 18th century formal gardens, and Ireland's largest, private contemporary art
collection, at every turn, The Merrion exudes the unmistakable air of timeless excellence.

There is nowhere finer to stay.

The
MERRION
DUBLIN

A member of
The Leading Hotels of the World®

Upper Merrion Street, Dublin 2, Ireland. Tel: 353 1 603 0600 Fax: 353 1 603 0700
e-mail: info@merrionhotel.com Website: www.merrionhotel.com

Mary McAleese
Building Bridges

Ambition and determination are two qualities that Mary McAleese has had instilled in her from an early age. When told by her family priest, that a girl could never become a lawyer, her mother was outraged. Telling Mary to ignore him, she promptly asked the priest to leave. Such early encounters with the constraints of convention have given Mary the drive to push the boundaries and unlock her inner potential.

Born Mary Patricia Leneghan on June 27th 1951 in Belfast, she grew up during the height of the Troubles as the eldest of nine children. Her father's shop was targeted in attacks and her brother beaten, during the unrest. Attending Saint Dominic's High School she later went on graduate from Queen's University Belfast with a law degree in 1973 and was called to the Northern Ireland Bar in 1974. 1975 saw Mary appointed as Reid Professor of Criminal Law, Criminology and Penology at Trinity College Dublin succeeding Mary Robinson, a pattern to be repeated 20 years later. In 1987 she returned to Queen's to become Director of the Institute of Professional and Legal Studies and later, in 1994, the first female pro-vice chair chancellor of the university.

Having also worked as a current affairs journalist and presenter through the medium of television and radio with Radio Telefis Eireann (R.T.E.), Mary McAleese has established herself as an experienced broadcaster. Other positions include Director of Channel 4 Television, Director of Northern Ireland Electricity and Director of the Royal Group of Hospitals Trust. With such versatility it is clear that this is a lady to whom a problem is merely a challenge that has not yet been scaled.

November 1997 saw Mary take on her most demanding role to date, becoming the eighth President of Ireland. Defeating the former Taoiseach Albert Reynolds during the election for the Fianna Fail presidency nomination, Mary went on to win the Presidency election with 58.7% of the votes. This appointment to President was particularly significant as it was the first time a female had ever succeeded another woman as an elected head of state, anywhere in the world. She also was the first President of Ireland that was actually born in Northern Ireland, adding yet another remarkable facet to Mary's journey.

The theme to Mary McAleese's presidency has been 'Building Bridges', a title that surely is apt for her journey so far. Concerned with such issues as justice, equality, social inclusion, anti-sectarianism and reconciliation, she epitomises all that defines a dynamic and forward thinking leader. At a time when new breath has been given to Ireland through an economic boom, this cosmopolitan and diverse country is clearly embracing its talent and allowing itself to grow. Mary McAleese has stated, "I believe we are an unstoppable nation, now very definitely in our stride." It is with such desire to unlock the potential from within that greatness can be discovered.

Mary McAleese
(opposite)

Samuel Beckett
Expression in Depression

"Nothing is funnier than unhappiness, I grant you that....
Yes, yes, it's the most comical thing in the world."

A Nobel Prize winner and one of the greatest writers of the 20th century. Yet unhappiness and pessimism were to form the core of Samuel Beckett's work.

Born in 1906 in a prosperous Protestant suburb of Dublin, Beckett was educated at Earlsfort House and at Portora Royal School in Enniskillen, where he excelled in modern languages. Indeed, much of his later work was written in French.

In 1923 he went to Trinity College, Dublin to read French and Italian. In Dublin he enjoyed the rich and vibrant theatre and cinema life. The silent comedies of Buster Keaton and Charlie Chaplin crucially influenced his interest in tramps.

After graduating in 1927, he taught in Belfast and then in Paris at the École Normale Supérieure. Here he was introduced to James Joyce. Beckett assisted Joyce in the construction of *Finnegan's Wake*, but also began writing himself. In 1930, he published his first poem *Whoroscope* and shortly after, the brief but groundbreaking, *Proust*. He returned to teach at Trinity but was unhappy and resigned. After the death of his father, he became depressed and unable to write.

He grew to dislike Ireland and once again left for Paris. In 1932, he wrote his first novel *Dream of Fair to Middling Women*, a highly autographical work and a powerful indication that Beckett was developing his own voice. During the next few years he moved continuously before settling in Paris in 1937. The following year *Murphy* was published - a novel about a young Irishman drawn towards madness. At around the same time, Beckett met Suzanne Deschevaux-Dumesnil and they were together until her death a few months before his own.

When the German occupation of France began, Beckett, although neutral, recognised the treatment of his Jewish friends and joined the French Resistance. However, his cell was betrayed and he and Suzanne fled to the village of Roussillion. They returned to Paris following the liberation. After the war, Beckett began to write in French. His trilogy of novels, *Molloy* (1951), *Malone Dies* (1951) and *The Unnamable* (1953) is among the greatest prose writings of the century.

Undoubtedly his most famous work is *Waiting for Godot*. The world of theatre was intrigued and bemused. Beckett himself regarded it as a liberating diversion from prose that had saved his sanity. Three more plays followed: *Endgame* (1958), *Happy Days* (1961) and *Play* (1963). In 1959, he received an honorary doctorate from Trinity College and in 1969, the Nobel Prize. His last major work, *Stirrings Still* was written in 1986. He died in December and was buried with his wife at the Cimetière de Montparnasse.

Beckett's satire can be biting and his wit devastating yet he found no escape from human tragedy, even in art. The depth of his thinking may be shocking but what he has to say is also comforting – a message delivered on courage, compassion and an ability to understand and forgive.

Samuel Beckett
(opposite)

W.B. Yeats
Master of the Mystical

From a fascination with Irish folklore to an obsession with the occult, William Butler Yeats is one of the greatest English language poets of the 20th Century. Between his Celtic visions of *The Wanderings of Oisin* (1889) and the often obscure, poetry of the 1930s, Yeats produced a tremendous amount of work during his career.

Born in Dublin into an Irish Protestant family, his father was John Butler Yeats, a well-known Irish painter. His early years were spent both in London and Sligo, which he later depicted in his poems.

In 1881, the family returned to Dublin for Yeats to study painting at the Metropolitan School of Art but he soon discovered he preferred poetry. Here, he met the poet, dramatist and painter George Russell, whose interest in mysticism inspired Yeats. Reincarnation, supernatural systems and oriental mysticism fascinated him throughout his life.

Yeats made his debut as a writer in 1885 when he published his first poems in *The Dublin University Review*.

Passionate about promoting Ireland's heritage, he became involved with the Celtic Revival Movement and his writing at the turn of the century drew extensively from Irish mythology and folklore.

In 1887 the family returned to London and in 1889 he met his great love, Maud Gonne, a woman equally famous for her nationalist politics as for her beauty. Although she married another man, she remained a powerful figure in his poetry. Through her influence Yeats joined The Irish Republican Brotherhood but was more interested in Celtic revival than political struggle. His co-study of Irish legends and tales was published in 1888.

In 1896, Yeats returned to live in Ireland and co-founded the Irish Literary Theatre, where he worked as a director. In 1912, he met Ezra Pound, who introduced Yeats to Japanese Noh drama, inspiring his plays. In 1916, he published *Easter 1916* about the Irish Nationalist uprising

In early 1917 he bought and restored a derelict Noman stone tower, which became his summer home and a central symbol in his later poetry. In the same year, at the age of 52, Yeats married Georgie Hyde-Lee, 26 years his junior. During their honeymoon, Georgie displayed a gift for writing and their collaborative notebooks formed the basis of *A Vision* (1925), a book of marriage therapy spiced with occultism. In 1923, he was awarded the Nobel Prize.

In 1932, Yeats founded the Irish Academy of Letters and in his final years he worked on the last version of *A Vision* and published *The Oxford Book of Verse*. Yeats died in France in 1939 and in 1948 his coffin was taken to Sligo, although there is doubt about the authenticity of the bones.

Yeats is not only remembered as a playwright but as an important cultural leader, deeply involved in Irish politics. His life-long interest in mysticism and the occult may have been off-putting to some readers, but he remained uninhibited in advancing his philosophy; and his poetry continued to grow as he grew older.

W.B. Yeats
(opposite)

Thomas Barnardo
Doctor of the Destitute

The name Barnardo is synonymous with orphanages. Yet today there is no such thing. Childcare experts now agree that children should grow up in a family environment rather than an institution. It was not so in Victorian times and Thomas John Barnardo's crusade, to rescue children from the streets, was one of the best-known social interventions in the last half of the 19th century.

He was born in Dublin in 1845 but other facts about his childhood are unclear. His schooling included parish day school and St Patrick's Cathedral School, Dublin. He was seen as a troublemaker and did not pass public examinations. Approaching his seventeenth birthday, he became a strong evangelical Christian and his commitment to social work strengthened. Wanting to become a medical missionary he set off to London to train as a doctor.

However, the London that Barnardo arrived in was riddled with unemployment, poverty and disease. Thousands of children slept on the streets. Barnardo threw himself into missionary work in the East End and became involved in the Ernest Street ragged school. In 1870 he opened his first home for boys in Stepney Causeway. One evening a young boy was turned away because the shelter was full. He was found dead two days later and from then on the home bore the sign 'No Destitute Child Ever Refused Admission'.

It wasn't until 1876 that he resumed his medical studies and sat his final examinations in Edinburgh. He registered as a medical practitioner in London and was elected a fellow of the Royal College of Surgeons, Edinburgh in 1880. His evangelical efforts took on a grand scale. In 1872, he set up a huge tent outside the Edinburgh Castle public house – and reportedly around 200 people a night professed conversion. In the space of seven years and still not 30, Barnardo had exploded onto the humane and evangelical scene.

A year later he married Syrie Louise Elmslie. As a wedding present they were given a 15-year lease on Mossford Lodge and he now saw the opportunity to open a home for girls. In 1873, 12 girls came to live in a converted coach house next to the lodge.

More hostels were opened and his ambitious plan to create a village Home for Girls was realized by 1880. However, Barnardo firmly believed that children should be with families and in 1886, he established the first fostering scheme.

All this work took its toll on Barnardo's health and by the age of 50, he had a heart complaint. Despite periods of rest, he died on 19th September 1905. At the time of his death there were nearly 8,000 children in the 96 residential homes he had set up and more than 4,000 children 'fostered out.'

As with other charismatic social entrepreneurs, Barnardo's work provoked gossip and speculation and it is said, of Barnardo himself, that he had no claim to the title of 'doctor'. However there is no doubt that Dr Thomas Barnardo left an indelible and extraordinary mark on the development of social care and practice with children and young people.

Thomas Barnardo
(opposite)

Anthony Cronin

Living as an observer within his own country and experiences, Anthony Cronin has reflected Irish life throughout his work. Drawing inspiration from the world around him, Cronin has produced literary works that not only sit well on the page but actually strike a chord within the hearts of the audience.

Anthony was born in 1928 in Enniscorthy Co. Wexford. He was educated at Blackrock, University College Dublin and King's Inns. The early 1950s saw Cronin establish himself as associate editor of the renowned monthly title *The Bell*, following which he became literary editor of the English weekly journal, *Time and Tide*. His talents, however, were not recognised only in Ireland. Anthony became visiting lecturer in English at the University of Montana between 1966-1968 and poet in residence at Drake University Iowa from 1968-1970.

Such positions show his versatility and ability to apply his knowledge and experiences to different fields and as a result bring his unique point of view to each. This is echoed in the fact that he has never limited himself to one genre. Cronin has established himself as a literary critic of considerable authority through such works as *A Question of Modernity*; a poet through a multitude of poems such as *The End of the Modern World* and *Letters to an Englishman*; a novelist by penning works such as *The Life of Riley* and a dramatist by creating *The Shame of It*.

He was later appointed cultural and artistic advisor to the Taoiseach. This was a position in which he sought to implement much of what he had earlier advocated during his time as celebrated weekly columnist for *The Irish Times* throughout the 1970s and 1980s. During his time as a columnist, he emerged as one of the few critical commentators in the land. As a result, his appointment to the role of Cultural and Artistic Advisor was a shock to many. However, in Ireland the classic way to silence a rebel has often been to give them a seat beside the chief.

This position enabled Cronin to work as a key element in the creation of Aosdana, The Heritage Council, Irish Museum of Modern Art and the Discovery Programme for Irish Archaeology. His dedication to the arts has not gone unnoticed. He has received the Marten Toonder Award for his contribution to Irish literature and has been bestowed with honorary degrees from the University of Ulster, Trinity College, Dublin, and the National College of Art and Design. In 2003 Cronin was elected as Saoi in Aosdana, an honorary distinction in the arts, which only five individuals can hold at any one time. Such honours exemplify the degree to which he has shaped the literary world to date.

Anthony Cronin himself states that, "The possession of literature is as important as the possession of language." His dynamic nature comes from the drive to secure literature as a cultural cornerstone, served by his fluency and dry wit. Rarely can one man capture the essence of life and entertain a society with its posturing and foibles. Anthony Cronin however, is that man.

Anthony Cronin
(opposite)

Chaim Herzog
Israel's Sixth President

Diplomat, soldier, scholar, politician, journalist, lawyer, legislator and sixth president of Israel – few could boast such a long and distinguished career as Chaim Herzog.

Born in Belfast in 1918, he was the son of the Chief Rabbi of Ireland who later became the Chief Rabbi of Israel. He grew up in Dublin, receiving a thorough Jewish education, while attending Wesley College. In 1935, at the age of 17, he emigrated to Israel to study and then went to Cambridge and London universities, where he earned his law degree.

When Herzog graduated in 1942 he embarked on a long military career. After the outbreak of World War II, he joined the British Army, serving as an intelligence officer. By the end of the war he had become head of intelligence, participated in the liberation of several concentration camps, identified a captured soldier as the Nazi leader Heinrich Himmler and held the rank of lieutenant colonel.

Immediately after the war, he returned to Palestine and joined the intelligence division of the Haganah. His intelligence experience during the war was seen as a valuable asset and he became head of the IDF Military Intelligence Branch. In 1947 he married and in July 1949, was appointed head of the Secret Services Commission. Between 1950 and 1954, he served as military attaché in Washington, rising to the rank of major-general before retiring in 1962.

Over the next two decades, Herzog combined a business career with public service, first as managing director of an industrial development group and later as a senior partner in a Tel Aviv law firm. During the Six-Day War and Yom Kippur War, he was chief military commentator for Israel Radio and became renowned for his balanced broadcasts which boosted the morale of the population. After the Six-Day War, he was called back to active service, as the first military governor of Judea, Samaria and East Jerusalem. His multifaceted career reached another milestone in 1975 when he was appointed, in particularly trying times, Israel's ambassador to the UN.

Herzog wrote a host of books on military history and was a sought after commentator on political and military affairs. His book *The Arab-Israel Wars* was published in 1982. The following year, he was sworn in as Israel's sixth president. Armed with impeccable English and a cosmopolitan attitude, Herzog traveled extensively and did much to enhance Israel's standing abroad. In May 1993, Herzog stepped down from the Presidency and devoted himself to speaking tours, journalistic commentary and to writing his autobiography *Living History: A Memoire*. Over the years he was very active in voluntary activity, and was awarded the Knight Commander of the British Empire (KBE) in 1970 and honorary doctorates from many universities.

As president, he saw the presidency as a symbol of the unity of people and an institution that is able to express the nation's deepest feelings, encompassing all ethnic communities, nationalities and beliefs. He brought the message of Israel proudly and capably to the international community, earning him recognition and respect. He died on 17th April 1997.

Chaim Herzog
(opposite)

Ernest Walton
Ireland's Einstein

In 1932 a scientific breakthrough at Cambridge University provided the world with atomic power and the first ever Nobel Prize for an Irish-born scientist.

Ernest Thomas Sinton Walton was born at Dungarvan, Co. Waterford on October 6th 1903, the son of a Methodist minister from Co. Tipperary. The demands of the ministry meant moving from place to place every few years which resulted in the young Ernest attending schools in Banbridge, Co.Down and Cookstown, Co. Tyrone. In 1915 he was sent as a boarder to Methodist College Belfast where he excelled in mathematics and science. In 1922, on a scholarship, he entered Trinity College, Dublin to read honours courses in mathematics and experimental science, specializing in physics. In 1926 he graduated with a first class honours in both subjects, receiving his MSc degree in 1927.

Shortly after, Ernest was awarded a research scholarship by the Royal Commissioners for the Exhibition of 1851 and began his career at Cambridge University working under Lord Rutherford in the Cavendish Laboratory. It was here that he met and collaborated with John Cockcroft in the building of a linear accelerator. Working on a shoestring budget they built the apparatus out of bits of petrol pumps, battery leads and glass cylinders. At the same time other countries were using high quality equipment and benefiting from better financial backing.

The method they used accelerated protons into a lithium target using extremely high voltages - a highly dangerous process. Some Swiss scientists had already lost their lives trying the same experiment with far superior equipment.

Yet, despite the odds against them, on April 14th 1932, Walton and Cockcroft succeeded in being the first scientists to split the atom – a dramatic step forward in science. The fact that the experiment worked at all was purely a direct result of Walton's great manual ability.

Walton was the first to see the reaction taking place and in his report wrote: "In the microscope there was a wonderful sight. Lots of scintillations, looking just like stars flashing out momentarily on a clear dark night."

Walton soon returned to Trinity College, Dublin where he was elected to fellowship in 1934. In the same year he married Freda Wilson, a daughter of a Methodist minister and also a former pupil at Methodist College Belfast and together they had four children, three of whom trained as physicists. In 1946, still at Trinity, he became Erasmus Smith's Professor of Natural and Experimental Philosophy – a rather grand title for Professor of Physics – and in 1960 he was elected Senior Fellow of Trinity College.

Outside his academic work, Walton took part in many activities and served on numerous committees including the Dublin Institute for Advanced Studies, the Royal Irish Academy and the Royal City of Dublin Hospital.

For his work with John Cockcroft in 1932, Walton jointly received the Noble Prize for Physics in 1951. It was the beginning of accelerator-based experimental nuclear physics which continues to teach us so much about the nature of matter today. Prof. Ernest Walton died in Belfast on June 25th, 1995. In his memory, the Walton Science and Technology Building at the Methodist College in Belfast is dedicated in honour of this remarkable 'old boy' of the school.

Ernest Walton
(opposite)

Percy French

'Where the Mountains o' Mourne sweep down to the sea.'

Whilst this may be the song for which he is best remembered, it is less well known that Percy French was also a talented artist, poet, actor and musician, as well as a song-writer.

William Percy French was born on May 1st 1845, at Cloonyquinn in Co. Roscommon. He was educated at Windermere College, Foyle College, and at Trinity College, Dublin, where he studied civil engineering. It was here that French focused much less on academic aspects and more on developing his artistic and creative talents. In 1877 he wrote *Abdulla Bulbul Ameer* for a college concert, which proved very successful.

After graduating in 1881, French planned to emigrate to Canada, but instead obtained the job of inspector of drains for the Board of Works in Co. Cavan. At this point he found time to enhance his interests in music and drama, writing famous songs such as *Phil the Fluter's Ball* and *Slattery's Mounted Fut*. Many of his songs, both humourous - *Are Ye Alright There Michael?* and poignant - *Come Back Paddy Reilly, To Ballyjamesduff*, were inspired by his own experiences. When he lost his job in 1887 he worked for two years as the editor of *The Jarvey* which was a weekly comic paper. He took advantage of this by using it to promote a series of concerts in Ireland under The Jarvey Concert Company.

But tragedy struck in 1891 when Percy's wife of one year, Ettie Armytage, died whilst in childbirth and, a few days later, their baby daughter also died. It is thought that this inspired his moving poems *Gortnamona, Not Lost But Gone Before* and *Only Goodnight*. Now without his wife and unemployed, French toured the country as a one-man show, singing the songs he composed. He also painted, finding inspiration in the rich Irish landscape. At this point he formed a partnership with Dr Houston Collisson, who would write the music for the operas they created such as *The Irish Girl* and *The Knight of the Road*. Indeed, some of French's later songs were written with music composed by Collisson - *Eileen Oge, Jim Whelehan's Automobeel, Donnegan's Daughter,* and *The Mountains o' Mourne* to name a few.

In 1892 French married Helen Sheldon and they had three daughters. He turned to the stage for his full time career. Along with his friend Richard C Orpen, the topical revue *Dublin Up To Date* was developed, forming the basis of a very successful stage entertainment career.

Having found fame in Ireland, French moved to London in 1900 aged 50.. He performed in the theatres and music halls of the major cities of Britain. London would be his base from now on. Possibly the peak of his career came in 1910 when French and Collisson toured the USA, Canada and the West Indies, all to great acclaim. During World War I he travelled through England and France, providing entertainment for the troops and raising money. Despite this, French never failed to return to perform in the towns of Ireland every year.

In 1920, whilst performing in Glasgow, French took ill. He died a few days later from pneumonia, on 24th January. He is buried in Formby, Lancashire.

Today, more than 80 years after his death, the memory of Percy French remains strong. The finest collection of his watercolour paintings is in The Percy French Society in The North Down Heritage Centre and a memorial doorway marks the site of his old home on Cloonyquinn. But it could be said that it is for his songs that Percy French will be best remembered, for the songs that have reached audiences throughout the world.

Percy French
(opposite)

Ernest Shackleton
Exploring Excellence

From a young age, Sir Ernest Shackleton knew he would become an explorer: *"I seemed to vow to myself that some day I would go to the region of ice and snow and go on and on till I came to one of the poles of the earth"*. In 1907, coming within 97 miles of the South Pole, he set a new record, before going on to lead one of the greatest tales of survival in expedition history.

The journey begins in 1874. Ernest was born into a farming family in Co. Kildare, at the time of the disasterous potato famine. His father, a survivalist, left for Dublin to study medicine. In 1884, the family crossed the water to settle in England. Although Ernest's father was keen for his son to follow in his footsteps, Ernest had other ideas. At the age of 16 he went to sea, travelling through the Far East and America. By the age of 24 he was certified as Master and qualified to command a British ship anywhere on the seven seas.

In 1897, Shackleton met Emily Dorman and, having had enough of sailing to the East, took a position with the Union Castle Line where he was able to come home regularly and pursue his love interest.

In 1900 Shackleton volunteered for Scott's National Antarctic Expedition and was chosen to go to the South Pole in 1901. However, he become seriously ill and was forced to return home. Once recovered, he was asked to take a ship to rescue Scott and dissuade him from spending another winter at the Pole. Shackleton declined, wanting to "prove himself a better man" with his own expedition.

In 1904 Ernest and Emily married and Shackleton discovered a new-found gift – public speaking. He made many acquaintances and was soon asked to run for Parliament but lost the election. A time of uncertainty was to prevail until 1907, when he led the record breaking Nimrod Expedition to the South Pole, resulting in a knighthood in 1909.

It was, however, his voyage to the Antarctic (1914 –1916) that truly demonstrated Ernest Shackleton's brilliant leadership ability. Just one day's sail from the continent his ship *Endurance* became trapped in sea ice. Frozen fast for ten months, the ship was destroyed and the crew forced to abandon her. After camping on ice for five months, Shackleton made two open boat journeys, one of which, a treacherous 800 mile ocean crossing to South Georgia Island, is now considered one of the greatest boat journeys in history. Trekking across the mountains he reached the island's remote whaling station, organised a rescue team and saved all of the men he had left behind.

Sir Raymond Priestly, who accompanied Shackelton on his Antarctic expeditions commented *"For scientific leadership, give me Scott, for swift and efficient travel, Amundsen; but when you are in a hopeless situation, when there seems to be no way out, get on your knees and pray for Shackleton."*

Shackleton's final goal was to circumnavigate the Antarctic continent, but suffering great mental and physical stress, he died on South Georgia Island in 1992, where his wife insisted he was buried.

Ernest Shackleton
(opposite)

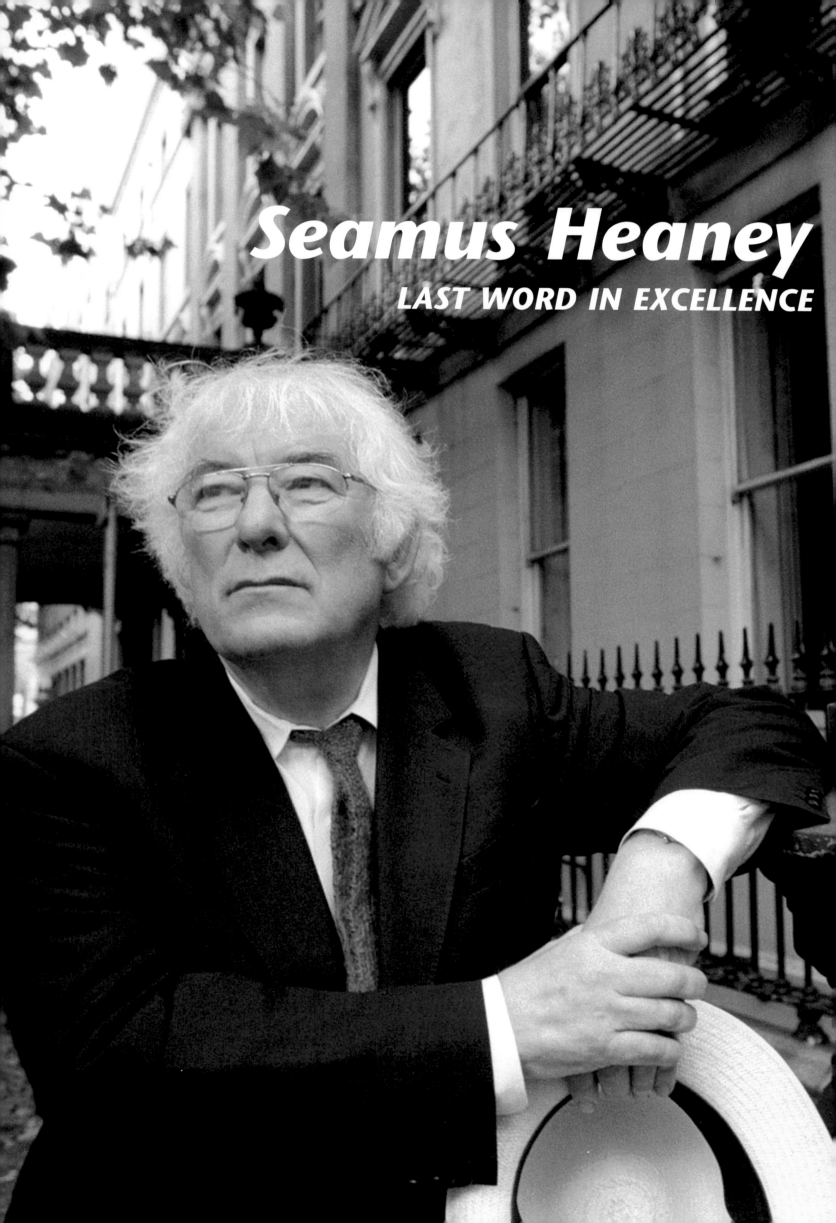

Seamus Heaney
LAST WORD IN EXCELLENCE

On April 13th 1939, Seamus, the first child of Patrick and Margaret Kathleen Heaney, was born on a farm called Mossbawn, Co. Londonderry, a name that has become mythical in his poetry, re-occurring time and again throughout a writing career that has spanned nearly 40 years.

As the eldest of nine, Heaney might have been expected to follow in his father's footsteps, becoming a farmer and cattle dealer. However his gradually discovered love of the English language was to take him into a different field. After attending the local primary school, Seamus won a scholarship to St. Columb's College, Londonderry and in 1957 entered Queen's University where he took a first in English in 1961.

It was here that Heaney began to write and the university magazines, *Q* and *Gorgon* published his first work under the pseudonym Incertus (i.e. Uncertain). The head of English at Queen's encouraged Heaney to apply to Oxford for postgraduate study, but, lacking what he later described as the confidence, the nous and the precedent, and feeling obliged to start paying his way, he chose instead to go to St Joseph's College in Belfast to train as a school teacher.

After just one year in his first teaching post, Heaney quit, following the offer of a lectureship back in St Joseph's. Here he met the English poet and critic Philip Hobsbaum, who was intent on bringing poets together, as he had done in London, for regular meetings. Along with Heaney and Hobsbaum, the circle of poets which included Michael Longley and Derek Mahon, became known as 'The Group'.

In 1964 Hobsbaum sent some of the group's poems to an old associate of the London group who, in turn, forwarded them to the literary advisors of various journals, amongst them Karl Miller, at the *New Statesman*. Miller was very taken with three of Heaney's poems - *Digging*, *Scaffolding* and *Storm on the Island* which were published in a single issue of the *New Statesman* in December 1964.

In 1965 Heaney married Marie Devlin and his first pamphlet *Eleven Poems* was published. It received good reviews including one by John Carey, who described three of Heaney's poems as 'masterly'.

The following year was no less significant. Heaney resigned from St Joseph's to become a lecturer in modern English Literature at Queen's, his first son Michael was born and Faber and Faber published *Death of a Naturalist*. The book earned him, amongst others, the EC Gregory Award in 1967 and the Geoffrey Faber Memorial Prize in 1968. His second son Christopher was also born in 1968.

In 1969 *Door into the Dark* was published, and became the Poetry Book Society Choice for the year. *Wintering Out* in 1972 followed. Heaney had spent the academic year of 1970-71 at the University of California at Berkeley and on his return gave up his job at Queen's to set up home in Co.Wicklow. He wanted, as he put it later, "to put the practice of poetry more deliberately at the centre of my life."

For the next three years Heaney made his living as a full-time writer. In 1973, when his daughter Catherine Ann was born, Heaney resumed teaching, taking up a post in Carysfort College, Dublin, in 1975. He moved to the city soon after and it has remained his home ever since.

1975 was also the year of *North*, his most political volume and his most criticised work. However, the book won the WH Smith Award, the Duff Cooper Memorial prize and was a Poetry Book Society Choice.

Two more works followed - *Field Work* in 1979 and in 1980, *Selected Poems and Preoccupations: Selected Prose*. In 1981 he left Carysfort to become a visiting professor at Harvard. In 1982 he won the Bennett Award and Queen's University conferred on him an honorary Doctor of Letters degree. In 1984 Heaney was elected Boylston Professor of Rhetoric and Oratory at Harvard and five years later, Professor of Poetry at Oxford.

However, of all his accolades, undoubtedly the most prestigious is the Nobel Prize for Literature, which Heaney was awarded in 1995 for 'works of lyrical beauty and ethical depth, which exalt everyday miracles and the living past'.

In recent years, Heaney has continued to produce numerous poems and writings including the much-admired translation of *Beowulf* in 1999, awarding him the Whitbread Prize. His version of a song cycle by Leos Janacek, *Diary of One Who Vanished*, has been staged by the English National Opera in London, Dublin, Paris, Munich, Amsterdam and New York.

From a humble farming community came one of our country's greatest writers who has demonstrated that poetry, like the land, is evidently something to be ploughed and turned over.

IRELAND AND THE EU

Ireland and the EU

European Union Flag
(above)

O n the 1st of May 2004, whilst under Irish presidency, the political and economic character of the EU was transformed with the expansion of the EU to 25 member states. The previous 15 members were Ireland, Austria, Belgium, Denmark, Finland, France, Germany, Greece, Italy, Luxembourg, The Netherlands, Portugal, Spain, Sweden and The United Kingdom. These members are now joined by 10 new members, Cyprus, Czech Republic, Estonia, Hungary, Latvia, Lithuania, Malta, Poland, Slovakia and Slovenia. This was the biggest enlargement ever of the EU and has resulted in a population of 455 million people within the EU. Negotiations for entry continue with Bulgaria and Romania. The European Council of Head of State of the 25 member states will decide, at its meeting in December 2004, on the possible opening of accession negotiations with Turkey. Croatia and Former Yugoslav Republic of Macedonia have also applied for membership of the community.

The European Union and its institutions developed in the aftermath of two devastating world wars. The founders envisaged a Union, formed on the basis of co-operation between sovereign states that would build a prosperous Europe in an environment of freedom and peace.

From left to right, Mr. Romano Prodi, President of the European Commission, An Taoisesch Bertie Ahern, President of the European Council and Pat Cox, President of the European Parliament
(opposite)

Ireland became a member of the European Union in 1973. The proposal to join the then European Economic Community was approved overwhelmingly in a referendum in 1972. Few could have foreseen then the enormous impact that membership would have on Ireland.

Ireland has experienced many great changes since joining the European Community. The phenomenal growth and modernisation of the Irish economy that we have witnessed has been greatly assisted by Ireland's membership of the Single European Market. In addition, the transfer of structural and cohesion funds has enabled the modernisation of the country's infrastructure, a process that continues to this day. Membership of the Union has resulted not only in European markets being open to Irish based firms but has also led to the attraction of foreign direct investment to Ireland from global firms that use their Irish bases as a springboard into those markets. The contribution of the union to halting and reversing emigration, in addition to virtually eliminating unemployment, cannot be overstated.

In other areas also membership has brought its benefits. EU consumer legislation has introduced some of the world's strongest consumer protection measures in diverse areas ranging from food safety to airline passenger rights. Indeed, the Food and Veterinary Office of the Union which enforces community legislation on food safety is based in Ireland, in Grange, Co. Meath.

Taoiseach Bertie Ahern President of the European Council joined by the member states 1st May 2004
(below)

**The flag raising ceremony
for 10 new member states
at Aras An Uachtarin,
1st May 2004**
(above)

The EU's competition laws have helped to free the Irish economy of many restrictive practices, to the benefit of consumers. The introduction of competition in air travel, telecommunications and several service industries has ensured the arrival of many new firms into previously monopolised industries. The result has been a dramatic fall in prices for many products especially in the air-travel and telecommunications sectors. The Union is determined to continue its policy of ensuring that a level playing field exists for all competitors and to monitor unfair and restrictive practices.

In social legislation also, the Union has made an enormous impact. Indeed, community legislation resulted in the introduction of equal pay for men and women in the mid-1970s. Since then, the Community has overseen the introduction of numerous social enhancement measures in the spheres of employment, health and safety at work, training and education, to mention just a few. The European Agency for the Improvement of Living and Working Conditions was established by Ireland's first European Commissioner, Dr Patrick Hillery and is based in Loughlinstown, Co. Dublin.

Environmental matters have become issues of great concern in Ireland over the past 30 years.

The Union's legislation on the environment covers many sensitive environmental issues. For example, European legislation seeks to ensure that air and water quality standards are maintained at the highest levels. Countries that fail to take measures to ensure compliance are liable to legal action by the Community.

After more than 30 years of EU membership, Ireland has been transformed from one of the poorest regions in Europe to one of the wealthiest. At the time of accession to the Community, Ireland's GDP per capita was approximately two thirds of the European average. Thirty years later, Ireland's per capita

GDP has raced ahead of all other Member States, except Luxembourg, to make it one of the most prosperous countries in the world. When placed alongside the elimination of emigration and unemployment, there can be little doubt of the impact that EU membership has had on Ireland. Indeed, in the increased Union of 25 Member States, it is hardly surprising that the new member states see Ireland as an example of how they too can make a success of EU membership.

Few could have anticipated these developments. Perhaps Ireland's economic performance within the EU can be best summarised by the words of former Taoiseach, Dr Garrett Fitzgerald delivering a Thomas Davis lecture in 2002.

"In retrospect, it is now clear that supporters of accession to the Community in 1972 actually under-estimated seriously the economic benefits of membership."

The Union is looking to the future and work to adopt a European constitution continues. In this context, the Union is also assessing its role in the world. The European Union is a unique experiment in co-operation between sovereign Member States. It is also a uniquely successful one. For more than 50 years it has achieved its principal ambitions of ensuring peace and stability between the states of Europe and greater prosperity for its citizens.

Everything you need to know

EUROPEAN COMMISSION REPRESENTATION IN IRELAND

Tel: **(01) 634 1111** Fax: **(01) 634 1112**
www.euireland.ie

Europe Direct: **00 800 6 7 8 9 10 11**
European Commission's Central Website: **http://europa.eu.int/comm**
Call to our Public Information Centre at 18 Dawson Street, Dublin 2

Groups, including school classes, are welcome - for arrangements phone **(01) 634 1111**

NORTH-SOUTH CO-OPERATION

North-South

The Belfast / Good Friday Agreement provides for new institutionalised arrangements for co-operation between Northern Ireland and the South. These include the North/South Ministerial Council, which brings together Ministers from the Northern Ireland Administration and the Irish Government, to take forward co-operation to mutual benefit. They also include new bodies which operate on an all-island basis under the direction of the North/South Ministerial Council, with clear accountability lines back to the Northern Ireland Assembly and Dáil Éireann.

The bodies are:

Tim O'Connor
Joint Secretary North/South Ministerial Council Joint Secretariat
(top left)

Dr. Peter Smyth
Joint Secretary North/South Ministerial Council Joint Secretariat
(above right)

The Agreement cover
(below)

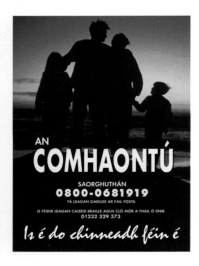

- *Waterways Ireland*

- *The Food Safety Promotion Board (FSPB)*

- *The Trade and Business Development Body (InterTradeIreland)*

- *The Special EU Programmes Body (SEUPB)*

- *The North/South Language Body (consisting of two agencies, Foras na Gaeilge and Tha Boord o Ulster-Scotch)*

- *The Foyle, Carlingford and Irish Lights Commission (FCILC) (which includes the Loughs Agency)*

Co-operation

In addition to the above, a publicly-owned limited company, Tourism Ireland Ltd, was established to market the island of Ireland overseas as a tourism destination. Tourism Ireland also operates under the direction of the North/South Ministerial Council.

The six North/South bodies and Tourism Ireland Ltd., represent a new partnership approach to taking forward co-operation between the two parts of the island. The focus is very much on tangible practical benefits to both parts of the island. Although only in existence since 1999, the bodies have achieved significant progress in delivering on their mandates and in demonstrating the value of North/South co-operation in terms of quality public services.

Much credit is due to the boards, management and staff for the success of the North/South bodies in fulfilling their remits. For those of us in the NSMC Joint Secretariat, it has been a privilege to work with and support them in fulfilling their mandates and we wish them continuing success in the future.

The Agreement cover
(below)

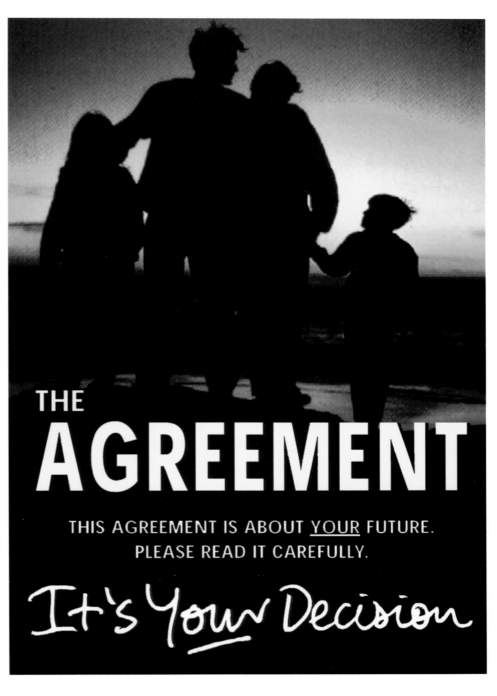

THE
AGREEMENT
THIS AGREEMENT IS ABOUT <u>YOUR</u> FUTURE.
PLEASE READ IT CAREFULLY.

It's Your Decision

Tourism Ireland
- an introduction

Marketing the island of Ireland Overseas

Tourism Ireland is the all-island body responsible for marketing the island of Ireland overseas as a tourist destination. Established under the framework of the Belfast Agreement of Good Friday 1998, the company has two goals:

- *To promote increased tourism to the island of Ireland*
- *To support the industry in Northern Ireland to reach its potential.*

Jointly funded by the two governments, South and North on a 2:1 ratio, Tourism Ireland has been fully operational since the beginning of 2002 when it launched an extensive programme to market the island of Ireland overseas as a tourist destination.

In addition to the company's primary strategic destination marketing role, Tourism Ireland also undertakes regional/product marketing and promotional activities on behalf of Fáilte Ireland and the Northern Ireland Tourist Board through its international market offices.

Tourism Ireland also owns and manages Tourism Brand Ireland (TBI) and all its associated communications materials. As a brand it is unique, in that, although Tourism Ireland is the promotional body carrying out the destination marketing, it does not own the product associated with the brand.

Partnership is the foundation stone of Tourism Ireland. Strong bonds of co-operation exist, not only between the complementary activities of the two tourist boards, but also between those bodies and all tourist enterprises, large and small, at home and overseas.

The tourism industry worldwide

Travel and tourism is the third biggest industry in the world, accounting for 693 million trips in 2001 and €516 billion revenue. Affordable access costs mean that consumers are now able to choose from an ever-growing range of diverse locations such as the Far East and the Americas.

The World Tourism Organisation (WTO) forecasts that the number of international arrivals worldwide will continue to increase from 696 million in 2000 to almost 1.6 billion in 2020.

The pace of change in the travel sector in terms of consumer demands, distribution systems and communications platforms, means there is a constant need to be innovative and creative regarding the promotion of Ireland abroad as a tourism destination.

Of all the recent developments, the internet is recognised as having the most profound effect on the travel sector. The global internet audience rose to 580 million at the end of May 2002 – an increase of more than 173 million since December 2002 (Nua). A record 94.3 million people worldwide visited a travel site in January 2002 (comScore) and current estimates for on-line travel spending are €20.4 billion (Jupiter Media Metrix).

www.tourismireland.com, the Tourism Ireland site, is a site of excellence for all visitors and potential visitors considering a holiday in Ireland, offering consumers a diverse mix of products both North and South.

Ireland as a tourist destination

The island of Ireland is a niche player in the world travel markets (1% market share: World Tourism Organisation). Ireland's closest competition includes destinations such as Scotland, England and Wales, Northern France and Scandinavia.

Around 80% of international visitors to Ireland come from four key markets: Great Britain, North America, France and Germany and almost seven million international visitors came to the island of Ireland in 2001.

The majority of current and potential visitors to the island of Ireland fall into the ABC1 category and consist of pre- and post-family adults. Well educated and much travelled, they are seeking an authentic experience. These visitors can broadly be broken down into those seeking self-drive or escorted touring visits, city breaks, special interest holidays, conference/incentive travel, or English language learning visits.

While touring remains the backbone of the tourism industry, Ireland has had some notable success in developing some high yield niches such as conferencing, business and more latterly, special interest holidays such as golf visits.

However, following a period of unprecedented growth in tourism for over a decade, the industry has recently faced one of its most challenging periods, which included the foot and mouth crises, post September 11, the war with Iraq and the SARS virus.

However, market intelligence reaffirms that the island of Ireland proposition and product are well received and Tourism Ireland will continue to capitalise on that to Ireland's best advantage.

So what is the appeal of Ireland to international holidaymakers? It is a complex interplay of factors that, at their most simple, can be summed up under the headings of **People, Place** and **Pace**. In surveys, visitors reveal that the combination of the warm, hospitable people, beautiful scenery and unspoilt landscape are what sets the island of Ireland apart from other destinations. Add a slower, more relaxed pace of life into the mix and you have the perfect place for a holiday.

Marketing the island of Ireland

The concept of adopting a formalised 'brand marketing approach' to selling Ireland had often been raised through the 1980s and 1990s by a variety of industry interests. This assumed special relevance as the Ireland tourism product has continued to change and evolve.

In actual fact, Ireland was a brand long before the concept even existed. Through film, folklore and word of mouth, an aura and personality was created around the island of Ireland that no amount of advertising could hope to match. The brand that is 'Ireland' has grown organically and in 2002 Tourism Ireland launched a new global advertising campaign, based on the following proposition:

'Discovering the Irish way of life (breathtaking landscape, friendly people and a relaxed pace of life) enriches you'.

It is Tourism Ireland's central mission to manage and develop that brand in all its rich potential via a strategic and comprehensive marketing programme that includes advertising, publicity, promotions to both trade and consumers, a strong internet development programme, information and literature, all designed to develop an appropriate image of Ireland.

As a holiday destination, the island of Ireland offers the benefit of an enriching experience based on the beautiful scenery, engaging people and a relaxed pace of life. The core brand values used to communicate the Ireland promise are centred on authenticity, real interaction, a living culture and a relaxed pace of life.

Ireland – a truly memorable experience

From the Giant's Causeway to the Ring of Kerry – the whole island of Ireland welcomes you!

You might not know how to find it yet, but it will find you. Your place in Ireland. It might be a mood that comes over you, all of a sudden, as you wander through the workshop of a candle maker in Oughterard, join in a traditional music session in Enniskillen, finish off the perfect round of golf in Kildare or enjoy a bracing walk through the panoramic landscape of the Sperrin Mountains. And the people you meet, with their curious tales, captivating conversation and unique way with a phrase – before you know it, they'll be having you in for a cup of tea and a chat.

Time may stand still in Ireland but, whatever season you arrive, there's always time for a special moment. And no matter where you go, there's a full choice of accommodation, restaurants and things to do. Every season brings its own wonders.

'There's a corner of Ireland with my name on it'.

Hospitality

Ireland is famous for its hospitality and you'll receive such a warm welcome here that you won't want to leave us!

History

In Ireland, the past is truly a living spirit. The island is steeped in history and no matter where you go, you will be surrounded by places of historical interest ranging from monuments, stately homes, tombs and castles to medieval monasteries and churches. This rich diversity of history offers a fascinating glimpse into Ireland's past.

Festivals and events

No matter where you are in Ireland, you are never far away from a special event or festival. If you can, plan your trip to coincide with one of the many events that interest you - your holiday will be even more memorable.

Culture

People are at the heart of Irish culture and the island has a strong sense of culture, no matter which part you visit. The cities and towns abound with theatres, including the Abbey and Gaiety Theatres in Dublin and the Market Place, Armagh. Music is everywhere you go, from the concert halls of the Belfast and Cork Opera Houses, to Wexford Opera Festival right down to the buskers on the street corners.

Sports and activities

Ireland is increasingly becoming a centre for international sporting events, for example, golf. Ireland is home to some of the world's top courses such as Royal Portrush and the K Club, where the Ryder Cup is being hosted in 2006. In all, there are more than 400 golf courses throughout Ireland.

Ireland

InterTradeIreland
TRADE & BUSINESS DEVELOPMENT BODY

Opening the island for trade

Too often on this island valuable commercial relationships go undeveloped or potential customers are overlooked. Too often a lack of knowledge is preventing business people from making the most of trading on the island.

By opening the island for trade and through equipping companies to achieve their goals, Inter*Trade*Ireland is helping to tackle these lost opportunities and is encouraging business to compete more effectively.

In the last year or two there have been several concrete examples of the business community on both sides of the border taking a fresh look at the opportunities available and making new connections. For instance, following an introduction from Inter*Trade*Ireland, Belfast's Harland and Wolff of *Titanic* fame, was awarded part of the contract to reconstruct the Ha'Penny bridge over the Liffey in Dublin. Now that really is bridge building at its best!

Helping this process is the fact that, physically, North and South are getting closer. It used to be the case that it was easier to get from Belfast to Brussels than it was to get to regional centres in the South. That's all changed. There are vastly improved motorway, rail and air links making the whole island more accessible for trade than it has ever been before.

Opening the island for trade and encouraging competition lies in everybody's interests. It brings greater choice, better services and new opportunities. Over the last 30 years, many potential business opportunities, particularly those of a cross border nature, were lost. Inter*Trade*Ireland believes that there is much to be done – and much benefit to be derived – from fully exploiting the opportunities for trade on the island.

**Dr Martin Naughton,
Chairman of
InterTradeIreland**
(below)

Liam Nellis, Chief Executive

InterTradeIreland

TRADE & BUSINESS DEVELOPMENT BODY

Some of InterTradeIreland's work includes the following:

TRADE DEVELOPMENT

The InterTradeIreland Acumen programme is a business development programme designed to stimulate cross-border trade amongst SMEs on both parts of the island. The two main types of support provided are consultancy and marketing/sales salary support.

FOCUS assists SMEs the length and breadth of the island to bolster their cross-border sales and marketing opportunities by placing high calibre graduates with the company and providing a comprehensive support and mentoring package tailored to meet specific business objectives.

Supplier Education Programme

The aim of this programme is to create business opportunities for SMEs in the all-island public procurement market which is worth over €13 billion annually. The programme will consist of a series of workshops to enhance the skills, expertise and efficiency of those who wish to target the public sector.

TRADE AWARENESS

Every year InterTradeIreland hosts and/or sponsors several award ceremonies to encourage and celebrate North/South business success stories. We also publish sector specific market analysis reports.

Awards

The All-Island Trade and Business Awards have quickly established themselves as one of the island's leading award ceremonies, recognising companies who excel in trading throughout the island. Past overall winners have included Dromore-based Graham Construction who have been responsible for helping to upgrade the Belfast / Dublin road link and Belfast-based consulting engineers Kirk McClure Morton.

The Innovation Awards were created to affirm excellence in the development of new products, processes and management systems. The competition, organised in association with Invest NI and Forfás, is now run on an all-island basis and aims to highlight the importance of R&D.

BUSINESS AND ECONOMIC RESEARCH

InterTradeIreland is also engaged in an ongoing process of research, which is providing policymakers and businesses with factual information on the island economy. A wide range of business and economic issues are being examined including biotechnology, air transport, construction, trade statistics, manufacturing productivity, entrepreneurship, supply chain management, public procurement and the retail services industry.

Jonathan Hegan, Senior Partner at Kirk McClure Morton, overall winner of the All-Island Trade and Business Award 2003

(above)

InterTradeIreland
TRADE & BUSINESS DEVELOPMENT BODY

equityNetwork

Promoting Private Equity to Accelerate Business Growth

EquityNetwork is a major InterTradeIreland initiative which is helping accelerate business growth across the island through the use of private equity funding. Empirical evidence demonstrates that companies financed by venture capital grow faster and are more competitive than their traditionally financed peers, but traditionally, venture capital uptake on the island has been low compared to the US or GB.

To address this, EquityNetwork is helping businesses to become investor ready by providing free access to experienced equity advisors who will assist companies to develop realistic business plans and direct them to appropriate funding sources.

EquityNetwork also hosts an annual private equity conference which is the largest gathering of investors and those seeking investment on the island and they also organise the All-Island Seedcorn Competition. The competition, which has a prize fund of €220,000 for the island's best business plans, aims to encourage entrepreneurs and investors to consider the benefits of venture capital for early stage developments.

Irish **Benchmarking** Forum

Chaired by InterTradeIreland, the Irish Benchmarking Forum operates in association with every other development agency on the island. The Forum encourages companies to learn more about and adopt benchmarking practices which are known to improve competitiveness.

SCIENCE AND TECHNOLOGY

FUSION is the first all-island network between industry and academia. The network enables knowledge and technology transfer across the island, supporting business innovation and increased capability.

FUSI♦N

Knowledge Transfer Across The Island

InterTradeIreland's FUSION initiative is set to create 130 new all-island company based technology transfer partnerships. Welcoming the news was Liam Nellis, Chief Executive of InterTradeIreland and InterTradeIreland's FUSION Manager Julie Jordan.
(below)

expertiseireland**.com**
THE ISLAND'S KNOWLEDGE PORTAL

Developed by InterTradeIreland and the Combined Heads of the Irish Universities, expertiseireland.com is the most advanced on-line portal of its kind in Europe. The site brings together innovators and those at the forefront of developing the knowledge economy with the objective of boosting R&D levels on the island by fostering greater links between industry and academia.

These are just some of InterTradeIreland's major activities but we are also involved in other activities including: Digital Island, competitiveness issues, partnership work with other agencies, the CBI-IBEC Joint Business Forum, supply chain management, MBAAI events and the Institute of Designers in Ireland Design Awards.

For more information on these or any of our activities please contact us on
0044 (0)28 3083 4100
or visit us online at
www.intertradeireland.com

EquityNetwork's third Private Equity Conference 2004, where Don Keough, former President of Coca-Cola was one of the keynote speakers
(above)

Contacts

INTERTRADEIRELAND		info@intertradeireland.com
ACUMEN	Willie Maxwell	info@acumenprogramme.com
		www.acumenprogramme.com
FOCUS	Julie Jordan	julie.jordan@intertradeireland.com
SUPPLIER EDUCATION PROGRAMME	Paddy Savage	paddy.savage@intertradeireland.com
ALL-ISLAND TRADE AWARDS	Pat McLoughlin	pat.mcloughlin@intertradeireland.com
INNOVATION AWARDS	Pat McLoughin	pat.mcloughlin@intertradeireland.com
POLICY RESEARCH	Eileen McGloin	eileen.mcgloin@intertradeireland.com
EQUITYNETWORK	Margaret Hearty	equity@intertradeireland.com
IRISH BENCHMARKING FORUM	Paddy Savage	paddy.savage@intertradeireland.com
		www.irishbenchmarkingforum.com
FUSION	Julie Jordan	julie.jordan@intertradeireland.com
EXPERTISEIRELAND.COM	Marion McAneney	marion.mcaneney@intertradeireland.com

safefood
Food Safety Promotion Board

A relatively young organisation, safefood, the Food Safety Promotion Board is part of a unique government structure created in the aftermath of the Belfast Agreement, which was signed on Good Friday, 1998. The body's main objective is to communicate with and inform the public about the importance of food safety issues.

Designed to bring about an acceptable method of addressing issues common to the North and South of Ireland, regardless of political boundaries or beliefs, six such bodies were formed, operating on an all-island basis. *safe*food is answerable to both the Minister for Health, Social Services and Public Safety in Northern Ireland and the Minister for Health and Children in the Republic of Ireland. This form of co-operation across political boundaries aims to benefit all on the island through the creation of a climate of co-operation and greater openness by jointly addressing areas of common interest.

Ireland's excellent reputation as a producer of wholesome, natural food and the nature of our tourism industry means that it is vital that our entire food chain strives to reach the highest possible standards from beginning to end. It is within this sphere that *safe*food operates, promoting good practice, commissioning research and offering support to producers and food retailers, as well as the general public.

Since its launch in November 2000, the organisation has faced a number of difficult political obstacles, but has managed to make considerable impact despite these issues. Proactive dissemination of the body's food hygiene and nutrition messages, using targeted communications to a variety of audiences, has been the cornerstone of *safe*food's activity.

*safe*food's mission statement summarises the body's field of operation and objectives as follows: *'To protect and improve public health, by fostering and maintaining confidence in the food supply on the island of Ireland, in partnership with others'.*

Advertising, media relations, education programmes and a very successful helpline have formed the basis of a sustained effort to raise public awareness of the body 's role and functions.

The *safe*food brand was created as the public face of the organisation and has achieved excellent penetration through a series of advertisements in the media.

An integrated advertising campaign entitled 'Reality Check' has been designed to get people to examine and re-evaluate their own approach to food safety practices and behaviour. The first phase of the campaign features two 30 second executions entitled 'Jenny's story' and 'Olivia's story'. The executions show the effects of the 'hidden' causes of food poisoning in the home and focus on the guilt you would feel if you accidentally harmed someone close to you.

However, the public is not the body's only audience and another measure of *safe*food's success to date is reflected in its success at fostering relationships with sister organisations, the various food providers and other relevant bodies.

Current safefood advertising campaign
(below)

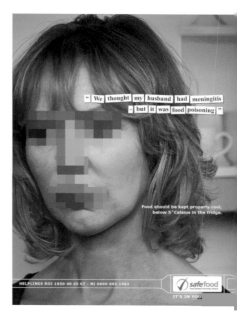

Schools Consultation Launch
Pupils at a Belfast school enjoy some fruit at the launch of the Schools Consultation, designed to give teachers the chance to voice their opinions about food safety and nutritional issues
(opposite)

safefood
Food Safety Promotion Board

"*Much of the work carried out by ourselves and our sister organisations, the FSAI (Food Safety Authority of Ireland) and the FSA (Food Standards Agency), involves reinforcing public confidence in the food we produce,*" says Martin Higgins, chief executive of *safe*food. "*Inter-organisation co-operation and clear communication can only serve to aid the public and industry alike.*

"*The choice of communication channel is vital if we are to become effective. In addition to the broad programmes outlined above, we must also be active at community level by supporting initiatives on the ground. Such an approach not only ensures accurate dissemination of our messages, but provides the two-way link that is at the core of effective communication.*

"*In the wake of BSE, the credibility of the food industry, academic institutions and government agencies has been seriously undermined. The communication of food safety and nutrition messages must therefore rely on solid scientific knowledge.*

"*safefood has a major role to play in contributing to this knowledge base. Through our work with producers, scientists and health professionals we will continue to work in partnership with others to advance specialist knowledge to help our food industry maintain and exceed its current standards of excellence.*"

Former NI Assembly Health Minister Bairbre de Brun launches the new all-island laboratory directory at Belfast City Hospital
(opposite)

safefood **Helpline Numbers**
Northern Ireland: 0800 0851683
Republic of Ireland: 1850 404567
Email: info@safefoodonline.com
www.safefoodonline.com

Northern Ireland comedienne, Nuala McKeever helps launch the Food Safety Week 'Calamity Kitchen Campaign'
(opposite page, bottom)

*safe*food staff demonstrate the dangers of cross contamination at the Balmoral Show, which attracts approximately 60,000 visitors each year

(below)

Foras na Gaeilge

Is é Foras na Gaeilge an comhlacht nua atá freagrach as an nGaeilge a chur chun cinn ar fud oileán na hÉireann. I gComhaontú Aoine an Chéasta dúradh go raibh Comhlacht Feidhmithe Thuaidh/Theas le bunú chun an Ghaeilge agus an Ultais a chur chun cinn. Faoi choimirce an chomhlachta sin, déanfaidh Foras na Gaeilge na freagrachtaí go léir i dtaca leis an nGaeilge a chur i gcrích. Áirítear ansin labhairt agus scríobh na Gaeilge sa láthair phoiblí agus phríobháideach i bPoblacht na hÉireann, agus nuair atá éileamh iomchuí i dTuaisceart Éireann i gcomthéacs Chuid III de Chairt Chomhairle na hEorpa um Theangacha Réigiúnacha agus Mionlaigh.

Tá foireann Bhord na Gaeilge, an Ghúim (Foilsitheoirí) agus an Choiste Téarmaíochta (Forbairt Téarmaíochta) agus a ngníomhaíochtaí ar fad aistrithe chuig an gcomhlacht nua.

Tá ról ag Foras na Gaeilge i dtaca le comhairle a chur ar riaracháin, Thuaidh agus Theas, chomh maith le comhlachtaí poiblí agus grúpaí eile sna hearnálacha príobháideacha agus deonacha i ngach gnó a bhaineann leis an nGaeilge. Ina theanta sin, déanfaidh siad tionscadail tacaíochta agus tabharfaidh siad cúnamh deontais do chomhlachtaí agus do ghrúpaí ar fud oileán na hÉireann. Áirítear i bpríomhghníomhaíochtaí an Fhorais:

- Eagraíochtaí agus gníomhaíochtaí Gaeilge a mhaoiniú
- An Ghaeilge a chur chun cinn (lena n-áirítear fógraíocht, comórtais, imeachtaí agus urraíochtaí)
- Treoirleabhair agus ábhar acmhainní a fhoilsiú
- Urraíocht a dhéanamh ar imeachtaí dátheangacha
- Ceardlanna agus seimineáir oiliúna
- Lainseálacha agus taispeántais
- Leabhair Ghaeilge agus leabhair inspéise ó thaobh na Gaeilge a tháirgeadh, a dháileadh agus a chur chun cinn
- Téarmaíocht nua don Ghaeilge a fhoirmiú agus foclóirí nua Gaeilge a thiomsú agus a fhoilsiú
- Tacú le hoideachas Gaeilge

Ná dearmad go bhfuil Foras na Gaeilge ann duitse agus, mar sin, má bhraitheann tú gur féidir linn cabhrú ná bíodh drogall ort teagmháil a dhéanamh linn. Tá an doras againn oscailte do chách.

Gaeilge

Foras na Gaeilge

FORAS NA GAEILGE is the new body responsible for the promotion of the Irish language throughout the whole island of Ireland. In the Good Friday Agreement it was stated that a North/South Implementation body be set up to promote both the Irish language and the Ulster Scots language. Under the auspices of this body, Foras na Gaeilge will carry out all the designated responsibilities, regarding the Irish language.

The responsibilities and staff of Bord na Gaeilge, An Gúm (Publishers) and An Coiste Téarmaíochta (Terminology Development) have all been transferred to the new body. FORAS NA GAEILGE is responsible for the promotion of the Irish language on an all–island basis. This entails facilitating and encouraging use of the Irish language as a living language in the South and similarly in Northern Ireland where there is appropriate demand.

Maighréad Uí Mháirtín
Chairperson
Cathaoirleach
(above)

To this end Foras na Gaeilge has a role in advising administrations, North and South, as well as public bodies and other groups in the private and voluntary sectors in all matters relating to the Irish language. Foras na Gaeilge will also be undertaking supportive projects and grant aiding bodies and groups throughout the island of Ireland

Foras na Gaeilge's main activities include:

- Funding Irish language organisations and activities
- Promotion of the Irish language (includes: advertising, competitions, events and sponsorships)
- Publication of guides and resource material
- Sponsorship of bilingual events
- Workshops and training seminars
- Launches and exhibitions
- Production, distribution and promotion of Irish language and Irish interest books
- Formulation of new terminology for the Irish language and the compilation and publication of new Irish language dictionaries
- Supporting Irish language education

Remember, Foras na Gaeilge is here for you so, if at any time you feel we may be of assistance, please do not hesitate to contact us. Our door is open to everyone.

Construction works on Royal Canal,
Co. Longford

Waterways Ireland
Uiscebhealaí Éireann   Watterweys Airlann

Ireland has a wealth of waterways with no commercial traffic to disturb their sense of peace and serenity. In total, over 1,000 kilometres of navigable rivers, lakes and canals link north, south, east and west. The connected network of inland waterways offers unrivalled opportunities to discover the real Ireland from a new and exciting perspective.

Background

Waterways Ireland - one of six North-South Implementation Bodies established under the British-Irish Agreement - is responsible for the management, maintenance, development and restoration of certain inland navigable waterways on the island of Ireland, principally for recreational purposes. The waterways under the remit of the body are the Barrow Navigation, the Erne System, the Grand Canal, the Lower Bann, the Royal Canal, the Shannon and the Shannon-Erne Waterway.

With its headquarters in Enniskillen and regional offices in Carrick-on Shannon, Dublin and Scarriff, Waterways Ireland is well placed to meet its responsibilities.

Waterway activities

Waterways Ireland promotes the waterways and the recreational opportunities available on them. As well as private boat owners using the waterway network, there are hire bases on the waterways offering cruisers and barges of all shapes and sizes. Boating is not restricted to cruisers and barges, with many types of sailing and power craft using the waterways in conjunction with water-skiers, rowers, canoeists, and jet-skiers.

On the banks are walkers and anglers and nearby sightseers also enjoying the riches of the waterways and the countryside. The waterways also comprise a mixture of historical, cultural, environmental, ecological and landscape elements, in and around which a wide range of recreational activities take place. Glorious scenery, together with a rich historic and environmental heritage, makes our waterways one of the world's most fascinating destinations.

In support of the various activities, Waterways Ireland produces a number of navigation charts and guides for the waterways offering a range of information on the practical use of the waterways as well as historical and environmental aspects. These are distributed all along the waterway system and are also available for sale in the Waterways Ireland offices.

Canoeists
(above)

A fisherman
(above)

Sailing
(opposite)

Cruising
(opposite)

Waterways Ireland
Uiscebhealaí Éireann   Watterweys Airlann

Development

Waterways Ireland is undertaking significant development work and is also implemented a programme of maintenance and improvement works on the waterways under its care. The Royal Canal which was abandoned in 1961 is currently undergoing restoration to complete the link back to the Shannon. When completed, a loop enabling boating from the Shannon to Dublin and back via a different route using the Royal and the Grand canals, will provide new and exciting recreational opportunities.

Other recent operational works have opened and improved navigations on the Shannon. The River Suck is now navigable all the way to Ballinasloe, while the completion of a new harbour near Boyle has created new interest on Lough Key.

The extension of the navigation on the Shannon through Limerick City has opened the previously short tidal constraints to enable a more leisurely approach to the centre of Limerick city than was previously possible. With new moorings and on-shore facilities the centre of Limerick has now the potential to welcome an extra 30 craft on short stay moorings.

The cross border link - the Shannon-Erne Waterway - has opened the Lough Erne system to the Shannon user and vice-versa, enhancing the potential of all the waterways. Its redevelopment added to the heritage associated with the inland waterways network and has brought further cultural heritage within the hinterland of the waterway network. Although the project was a major engineering undertaking and required significant investment, the tourism and environmental benefits of its restoration are clear to all. The increased tourism business has enhanced the local economy and a greater awareness and appreciation now exists of the heritage aspects, both physical and natural, of the waterway and the surrounding landscape.

Royal Canal restoration
(above)

Waterways Ireland Visitor Centre
(opposite)

Visitor Centre

The Waterways Ireland Visitor Centre is situated in a modern building on the Grand Canal Basin

in Ringsend, in the south-east of Dublin city. The centre houses an exhibition which explores Ireland's inland waterways, their historical background and their modern amenity uses. The display, which includes examples of art and literature inspired by the waterways and models of important engineering features, highlights the significance in today's world of a network of inland waterways developed some 200 years ago.

Ireland's inland waterways act as an important catalyst for regeneration in both urban and rural areas, supporting new and existing businesses and providing employment. From Coleraine in the north to Waterford in the south and from Dublin in the east to Limerick and Belleek in the west, the impact of the work of Waterways Ireland is experienced and the ripple effects of its actions are felt by communities throughout the island.

So why not get out – enjoy the waterways. Because…

Loughs Agency

Loughs Agency is an agency of the Foyle Carlingford and Irish Lights Commission, whose responsibilities relate to aquaculture and marine matters. It is one of the cross-border bodies established under the framework of the Belfast Agreement of Good Friday 1998.

The border which divides the two jurisdictions on the island of Ireland begins and ends in two sea loughs, Carlingford Lough in the East and Lough Foyle and the West. It is the Loughs Agency's responsibility to conserve, protect, manage and develop these loughs and the catchments which feed them in respect of the salmon and inland fisheries, the aquaculture and shellfisheries and for marine tourism.

The predecessor of the Loughs Agency was the original cross border body, the Foyle Fisheries Commission which was established in 1952 by two Acts, The Foyle Fisheries Act (Northern Ireland) 1952, which was enacted by the Stormont Parliament, and the Foyle Fisheries Act 1952, which was passed by the Oireachtas. These virtually identical pieces of legislation recognised that the resources of a cross border river basin could only be conserved, protected and developed if its management was harmonised in both jurisdictions. This far seeing, pragmatic and consensual approach has allowed the Foyle catchment and its salmon population to survive the impacts of 20th century human living better than most of the catchments in the North Atlantic inhabited by North Atlantic salmon.

The lessons learnt over the nearly 50-year life of the Foyle Fisheries Commission are being brought to the functions and responsibilities of the Loughs Agency and are perhaps encapsulated in the agency's mission statement.

"The Loughs Agency aims to provide sustainable social, economic and environmental benefits through the effective conservation, management, promotion and development of the fisheries and marine resources of the Foyle and Carlingford areas."

The salmon and inland fisheries stocks of the Foyle and Carlingford area sustain high quality recreational fisheries with an estimated annual catch of 10,000 salmon. There are also important and valuable commercial fisheries for salmon operating in the tidal reaches and sea area of the Foyle. These commercial fisheries have a relatively stable five year running average annual catch of 35,000 salmon. Both the recreational and commercial fisheries provide important sources of income to the region and so it is vital that these are well managed. The management regime, which the agency operates, aims to optimise the salmon resource and is built around the concept of sustainability and the importance of protecting stocks for future generations. The agency, through legislation, can close the fisheries for periods if stocks are low, thereby ensuring enough salmon are allowed to spawn at the end of each season in order to maintain these important fisheries.

The information which this management is based on relies on scientifically based monitoring and auditing of the stocks. The young salmon in the rivers are monitored throughout their time in freshwater with techniques such as electrofishing. These establish the abundance of these salmon in the streams and rivers of the Foyle and Carlingford areas and allow the agency to target areas with necessary works to improve the numbers of fish. The adult salmon, on their return to their native rivers after feeding at sea, are monitored at various stations with the use of electronic fish counters. In addition to these audit points, an ongoing genetic programme will, we hope, provide additional information, which will aid in the further development of new and innovative management techniques.

The River Finn
(left)

Greencastle Carlingford Lough
(above)

While the agency awaits the formalisation of primary legislation to enable it to fulfil the responsibilities given to it under the Good Friday Agreement, to extend its functions to include aquaculture and shellfisheries, it has developed a programme of scientifically based monitoring and audit. This will inform and direct the decisions required to protect and develop this varied resource towards optimal, but sustainable, productivity, on a similar basis to that operating for the salmon and inland fisheries of the catchments.

Historically, loughs Foyle and Carlingford had famous and prolific flat oyster (ostrea edulis) fisheries. For hundreds of years both loughs had been noted for their oysters. Carlingford's produce especially, was regarded as superior to all other oysters sold at the fish markets in Dublin and England. Over time, due mainly to over-fishing, the oyster populations in both Loughs declined. It proceeded to the stage where the commercial oyster fishery in Carlingford collapsed. Some native oysters can still be found in Carlingford and there is an ambition to establish a commercial flat oyster fishery there again. Lough Foyle, on the other hand, still has a significant native oyster fishery. It is a very important fishery as it is one of the last disease-free stocks of flat oyster left in Europe. The local oyster fishermen have developed a code of practice in conjunction with the Loughs Agency to protect this important natural resource and develop it to increase the population to its maximum sustainable level, which is the objective for the varied and valuable fisheries in both loughs.

With the decline in the oyster fishery came diversification. Mussels were the choice of the fishermen because the seed for on growing was plentiful and they grew to market size in half the time it took an oyster. Today, both loughs are producing sustainable amounts of mussels and the figures are increasing annually. The produce from both Loughs is regarded as a premium product on the European market and the price they command reflects this.

The loughs at present are producing significant quantities of shellfish and also generating substantial economic benefits to the local communities. It is the agency's objective to support and encourage the sustainable development of these fisheries and protect the high quality environment that they need to thrive.

As part of this process of sustainable development for both the shellfisheries and the inland fisheries of the areas, the agency believes that the communities of the catchments should have the opportunity to become more aware of the wonderful and varied resources they have, and with this in view *Riverwatch* has recently started to operate.

Riverwatch is the Loughs Agency's interpretive centre and is located in the headquarters on the banks of the Foyle. It is a unique educational resource and tourist attraction available to schools, communities and business organisations from all over Ireland and Britain. Its aim is to ensure the environmental survival and to maintain and develop the economic benefits of the Foyle and Carlingford waterways through increasing the level of knowledge of those directly and indirectly using its resources.

Riverwatch has three main goals:

• To act as a focus and source of information.;
• To raise environmental awareness of the general public of the natural resources of the loughs; and
• To inform the public of the social, environmental and economic resources of the loughs and their tributaries.

Carlingford Lough
(above)

The interpretive centre houses state of the art, multi-media installations and first class displays. A range of stories are told using local footage from the Foyle and Carlingford area including: the amazing life cycle of the salmon; angling; shellfish; habitats; protection; conservation; water quality; and, commercial fishing.

The target audience of *Riverwatch* are the stakeholders of the loughs. To date, *Riverwatch* has welcomed over 5,000 visitors from a range of backgrounds including, primary and post-primary schools, universities, government departments, angling clubs (including juvenile clubs), community groups and a local and international tourists. The feedback so far has been positive with comments such as:

"Thought provoking, educational and impressive facilities"

"First class – very educational"

"I enjoyed it and learnt a lot. I highly recommend it"

"Excellent educational resource"

"Brilliant presentations and very informative"
"Pleasantly surprised!"

Riverwatch, through the interpretive centre and the programmes and activities it offers, will not only help the agency to fulfil its responsibilities for the stewardship of the catchments but also expose the opportunities that there are for the public to enjoy their wonderful resources.

As indicated above, the agency also has responsibilities for the development of marine tourism within the areas. In this regard the agency is proceeding on a similar basis as with its other responsibilities by developing partnerships with the stakeholders, interest groups and those who influence the resources of the Loughs.

The agency is developing its strategy for the development of Mourne tourism in partnership with the local county and district councils in the areas through the North-West Region Cross Border Group representing Donegal, Derry, Limavady and Strabane councils and the Eastern Region Cross Border group representing Newry and Mourne, Down, Banbridge, Craigavon, Louth and Monaghan councils.

Together, these organisations are undertaking an audit of the existing resources and developments within the loughs with the objective of identifying the opportunities for further investment, co-operation and enhancement of the facilities to improve the economic, social and environmental benefits that can flow from them.

The agency is building on the consensual, pragmatic and far-seeing example of those who established its predecessor and of the concepts of the Good Friday Agreement to protect the resources of the catchments and encourage their sustainable development.

School children monitoring local stream
(left)

Fly fishing for bass in Carlingford Lough
(below)

Tha Boord o **Ulstèr**-Scotch
Ulster-**Scots** Agency

Ulster-Scots Agency

How often have you used the word craic, believing it to be Irish? In fact when using this word you are actually speaking Ulster-Scots, or Ullans as it is known today. Words are often borrowed from one language to another. This can occur for many reasons, for Ulster it was the fact that many Scots settled in the area.

Highland dancers and Lambeg drum player
Willie Drennan at an East Belfast Ulster-Scots awareness week. September 2003
(below)

For centuries tens of thousands of Scots crossed the narrow channel from Scotland to settle in Ulster. Their language was neither Gaelic nor English; instead they spoke a Germanic language. From this interaction Ulster-Scots was born, and so became interwoven into the unique tapestry of Ulster's vibrant culture.

Good Friday, April 10th 1998, marked the birth of The Ulster-Scots Agency, which is one of six cross-border bodies, produced as a direct result of the Belfast Agreement. Its aim may seem simple, to promote and develop the Ulster-Scots language and culture. In reality, promoting a language and culture widely viewed as 'poor English' in the classroom, and often the object of social prejudice, is a mammoth task. Its aim, to develop the public's understanding of Ulster-Scots, has been given a voice through the agency's initiatives. An Ulster-Scots language column has been introduced into the *News Letter* by the Agency for the first time. Alongside this, the Agency publishes a newspaper called *Ulster-Scot* and has developed a website to aid the public's understanding of both the language and culture.

During the plantation of Ulster between 1610-25 English became the language of choice for commerce, government and writing. This in turn relegated Ulster-Scots and Irish to the countryside and home. Outsiders living only a few miles away may never hear it, as conversations outside such communities are usually spoken in English. It does however remain a medium of daily life especially in four counties - Down, Antrim, Londonderry and Donegal. Ulster-Scots' origin is shared with English and the two have influenced each other

Welcome to the **Ards** Borough

Fair Fa'Ye
Tae the Airds

Area of Outstanding Natural Beauty

Ulster-Scots sign
Newtownards

Tha Boord o **Ulstèr**-Scotch
Ulster-**Scots** Agency

within the Province. As a result, it is often difficult to draw a sharp boundary of structure and vocabulary between Ulster-Scots and Ulster-English. This blurred divide has been unclear until now. The Ulster-Scots Agency is aiming to give a clearer understanding of the history of Ulster-Scots and aims to preserve it as a culture through various courses in areas such as music, language and the arts.

The agency believes that, only through the promotion of the language and culture in tandem, can Ulster-Scots be understood and preserved. It is through a number of grass-root activities in Northern Ireland, Donegal, Cavan and Monaghan that this conservation is taking place. The escalation of interest and activity in the Ulster-Scots movement has been so spectacular that its renaissance has become one of the most dynamic and dramatic cultural and linguistic revivals in post-nationalist Europe.

Jacob Thompson (7)
with a collection of Ulster-Scots writing, *Blad O Ulster - Scotch*, which was launched April 2004 with agency funding
(above right)

Ballinmore Primary School with John Coulter,
One of the winners of last year's Ulster - Scots schools cup.
(below)

One of the most striking results of the fusion between the Ulster and Scottish language and culture has been the creation of a vast melting pot of music and the arts. A prominent example of this has been the poetry of Robert Burns. A great connection was established between Burns and Northern Ireland in 1786 when extracts from the first edition of the *Kilmarnock Edition* were printed in the *News Letter*. It was the first newspaper in Ulster and possibly even the British Isles to do so. His poetry subsequently appeared frequently in the newspaper. Many pieces were published by the 'Ayrshire ploughman' before they even appeared in any collection of his works. The influence of Burns in Ulster was so great that it has been claimed that often only two books were present in an Ulster home, The Bible and a copy by Burns. Many of the old copies of Burns' work present in Ulster do not contain a glossary. This is due to the fact that many of the Scots words were so prevalent in Ulster that they needed no explanation.

Music has also thrived in Ulster from the introduction of Scottish culture. For example, the fiddle was first introduced into Ireland from Scotland through the Ulster-Scots, as was the dance form, the reel. However, it is not only Ulster that has benefited from such musical influences. The quarter of a million Ulster-Scots emigrants that travelled to the New World during the 17th century introduced many aspects of their culture. Dance and music styles originating from the Ulster-Scots culture can be found within that of the dance of the Appalachian region and country, bluegrass and folk music. Johnny Cash, George Hamilton IV, Ricky Skaggs and Dolly Parton all have links to the Ulster-Scots emigrants. Dolly's father, Robert Lee-Parton, had strong Ulster-Scot roots that can be traced back to the early settlers that travelled from the north of Ireland. She is so proud of these roots that she has even dedicated part of the musical documentary shown in her theme park to the Ulster-Scot influences.

Other high profile American Ulster-Scots include the world acclaimed author Mark Twain who wrote such classics as *The Adventures of Tom Sawyer* and *The Adventures of Huckleberry Finn*. Celebrated American frontiersmen David (Davy) Crockett, David Daniel Boone and Sam Huston were descendants of Ulster-Scot emigrants. However, most remarkable of all, is that 17 of the 43 American presidents have Ulster ancestry, including Andrew Jackson, Woodrow Wilson and Ulyssess Simpson Grant, Bill Clinton, George Bush, Richard Millhouse Nixon and Theodore Roosevelt. A further point that highlights the Ulster-Scot influence within America is that the original American Declaration of Independence was signed by only two persons both of whom, Charles Thomson and John Hancock, were Ulster-Sots. Such Ulster-Scot settlers are known in America as Scotch-Irish, however in Britain this has been avoided. This is not due to political or economic reasons; instead it has been set aside due to the link it holds with the alcoholic drink.

It is clear that the threads of Ulster-Scot culture are woven through politics, religion, commerce, industry, education, technology, music, journalism, literature, the arts, entertainment, mannerism and general attitudes to life. Not only in Ulster but further afield, particularly in the USA, Canada and New Zealand.

The Ulster-Scots Agency is striving to conserve this language. The agency has seen a demand for grants increase from four in its first year of operation to 305 for 2003. Its journey has only just begun but, with the tenacity and determination deeply embedded within its culture, it is sure to succeed.

For more information you can reach us at **www.ulsterscotsagency.com**

George Patton
CEO
(above)

Eamonn O' Cuiv
at Stormont
(below)

Special EU Programmes Body
Foras Um Chláir Speisialta An Ae

The Special EU Programmes Body

The Special EU Programmes Body is a North-South Implementation Body sponsored by the Department of Finance and Personnel in Northern Ireland and the Department of Finance in Ireland. The body was established under the Good Friday Agreement and the British-Irish Agreement establishing implementation bodies. The body reports to the North/South Ministerial Council.

The Special EU Programmes Body's principal functions are to manage certain EU Structural Funds, such as the EU Programme for Peace and Reconciliation (PEACE II), INTERREG IIIA Programme and other community initiatives and to support a range of development and regeneration programmes in the North and South of Ireland.

Sharing expertise and promoting economic development is the Fermanagh Leitrim Organic Co-Operative
(above right)

The Ballymena-based Can Can project, funded by the PEACE II Programme
(below)

The PEACE II Programme

The € 707 million PEACE II Programme aims to promote peace building and reconciliation. Projects funded by the programme must address the legacy of the conflict and take opportunities arising from peace, thereby promoting a stable and peaceful society. Thousands of projects have now been supported by the programme in hundreds of communities in Northern Ireland and the Border Regions of Ireland.

The INTERREG IIIA Programme

The INTERREG Programme is designed to support cross border co-operation, social cohesion and economic development between the regions of the European Union. The Ireland/Northern Ireland INTERREG IIIA Programme covers all of Northern Ireland and the six border counties of Ireland. The € 179 million programme aims to address the economic and social disadvantages which can result from the existence of a border, by promoting the creation of cross border networks involving, and also benefiting, local communities.

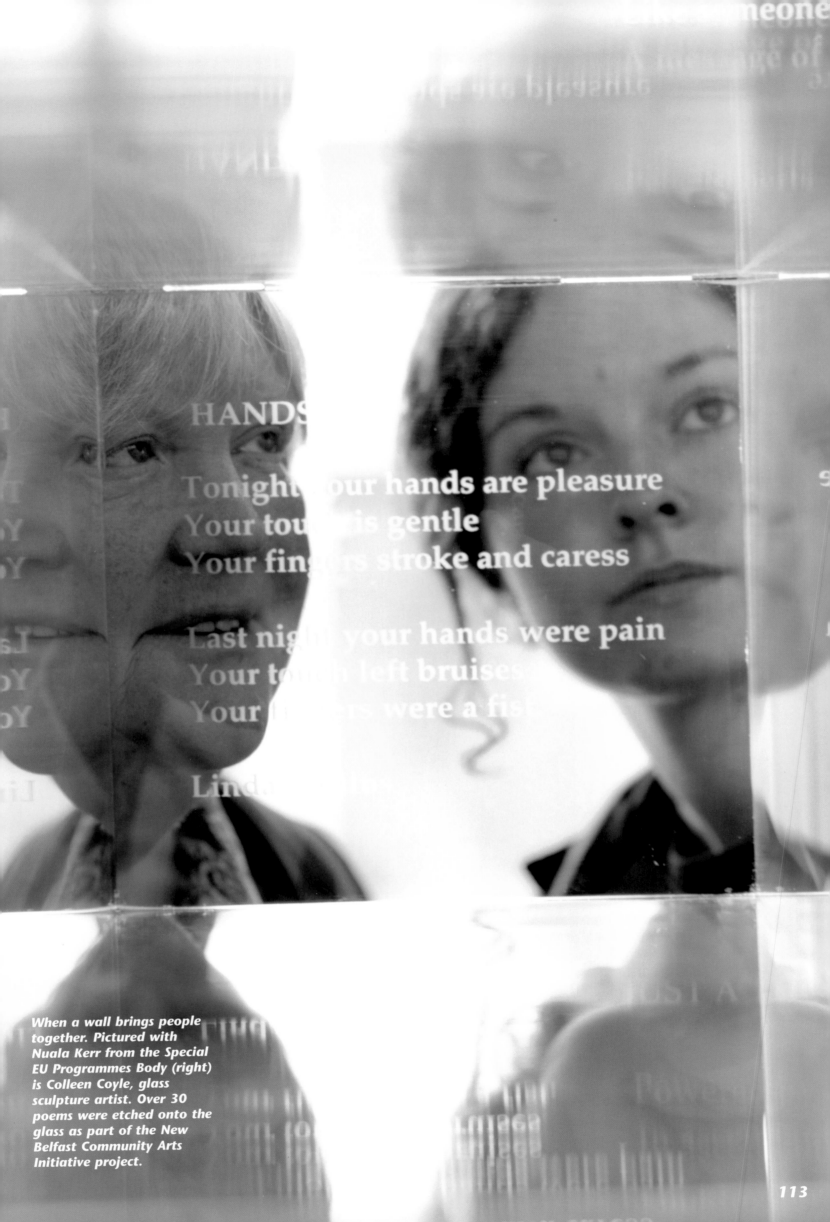

HANDS

Tonight your hands are pleasure
Your touch is gentle
Your fingers stroke and caress

Last night your hands were pain
Your touch left bruises
Your fingers were a fist

Linda

When a wall brings people together. Pictured with Nuala Kerr from the Special EU Programmes Body (right) is Colleen Coyle, glass sculpture artist. Over 30 poems were etched onto the glass as part of the New Belfast Community Arts Initiative project.

IRELAND'S
SPECIAL OLYMPICS

2003 Special
World

Olympics Summer Games

Ireland had never seen such a momentous sporting event as the 2003 Special Olympics World Summer Games. This great occasion was being hosted outside USA for the very first time since its inception in Chicago in 1968 and it kicked off, in spectacular fashion, with an exciting opening ceremony in Croke Park on 21st June.

Right from the start it was obvious that this was to be a unique event. The numbers involved in participation, coaching, officiating, volunteering and supporting were going to make impressive reading.

There were 7,000 athletes, 3,000 coaches and officials, from over 160 international delegations, all accompanied by many thousands of family members and friends. Over 30,000 volunteers were recruited, in Dublin alone, to ensure the games' success. Thousands of others were on hand across the

Olympic flame lit during opening ceremony
(opposite)

Muhammad Ali
during 2003 Special Olympic World Games
(below)

117

Special Olympics athlete Noreen McCarthy, photographed with actor Colin Farrell

whole of the island to assist with the Host Town Programme, ensuring the visiting delegations experienced the very best of Irish hospitality.

Almost 80,000 spectators attended Croke Park for the opening and closing ceremonies on June 21st and 29th respectively, while more than 2,000 members of the Garda Siochana and the Police Service of Northern Ireland (PSNI) took part in the Law Enforcement Torch Run. This series of relays saw the 'Flame of Hope' carried from Europe to the opening ceremony.

The Games' Organising Committee chose the theme 'Share the Feeling'. Their chairman, Mr Dennis O'Brien, stated that they wanted every single person on the island of Ireland to be part of this unique occasion. This was most certainly to the fore with the Host Town Programme, sponsored by premier sponsor, Bank of Ireland, which saw visiting delegations spend four days prior to the games

in an Irish Host Town. Over 160 communities came together to embrace this concept and give competitors an opportunity to train and relax prior to the competition.

The 'Support an Athlete' programme, sponsored by RTE, gave small companies and individuals the opportunity to become personally involved, to ensure athletes were able to perform to the best of their ability during their stay in Ireland.

Special Olympics athlete
Ruth O'Mahony Jnr
is embraced by her mother
(above)

Special Olympics athlete
Christopher Stocks
competes on the rings
(above left)

Special Olympics athlete
medal winners
(below)

There were also two family-centred programmes supported by Toyota: 'Host A Family Programme" and 'Family Ambassador Programme', which were designed to provide a cultural exchange between local families in the greater Dublin area and families from all over the world.

A Schools Enrichment Programme, sponsored by An Post, was used to promote awareness within schools and colleges of the skills and talents of people with learning disabilities.

These were just some of the many programmes and initiatives which were designed to create a lasting legacy for people with a learning disability following the games - a true value of Special Olympics. The island of Ireland made an important contribution to Special Olympics and global attitudes by hosting the 2003 World Games. We experienced the feelings of hope, optimism and pride that this unique event inspired.

SONGS, POETRY, PEOPLE AND PLACES

A selection of songs, poetry and quotes that portray an alternative view of the special beauty that is Ireland.

Cor ur

Cathal Ó Searcaigh

Ciúnaíonn tú chugam as ceo na maidine
mús na raideoige ar d'fhallaing fraoigh,
do ghéaga ina srutháin gheala ag sní
thart orm go lúcháireach, géaga
a fháiltíonn romham le fuiseoga.

Féachann tú orm anois go glé
le lochanna móra maorga do shúl
Loch an Ghainimh ar dheis, Loch Altáin ar clé,
gach ceann acu soiléir, lán den spéir
agus snua an tsamhraidh ar a ngruanna.

Agus scaoileann tú uait le haer an tsléibhe
crios atá déanta as ceo bruithne na Bealtaine
scaoileann tú uait é, a rún mo chléibhe,
ionas go bhfeicim anois ina n-iomláine
críocha ionúine do cholainne

ó Log Dhroim na Gréine go hAlt na hUillinne
ón Mhalaidh Rua go Mín na hUchta,
thíos agus thuas, a chorp na háilleachta,
gach cuar agus cuas, gach ball gréine,
gach ball seirce a bhí imithe i ndíchuimhne

ó bhí mé go deireanach i do chuideachta.
Tchím iad arís, a chroí, na niamhrachtaí
a dhearmadaigh mé i ndíbliú na cathrach.
Ó, ná ceadaigh domh imeacht arís ar fán:
clutharaigh anseo mé idir chabhsaí geala do chos,
deonaigh cor úr a chur i mo dhán.

Cathal Ó Searcaigh

A New Take

Translation: Cathal Ó Searcaigh and Nigel Mc Laughlin

Softly you come to me from the morning mist,
musk of bog-myrtle on your heather cloak,
your limbs' bright streams lapping gently
around me, limbs that greet me excitedly
with the tremulous soar of skylarks.

You see me truly
in the clearness of your big lake-eyes;
Loch an Ghainimh on the right, Loch Altáin on the left;
both stilly blue, full of sky;
the healthy glow of summer on their hilly brows.

And you loosen to the mountain breeze
your May-time veil of heat-gaze;
you loosen it, my love, you cast it off
that I may wholly see
the beloved boundaries of your body,

from Loch Dhroim na Gréine at the hollow
of your back to Alt na hUillinne's elbow bend;
from Mín na hUchta, the valley of your breast
to the red slope of your cheeks at Malaidh Rua.
My eyes slide over the hollows and curves of your beauty.

All those sights I had forgotten in my wanderings.
But I know what the city lacks
And I pray for an end to exile, for shelter
here between the bright paths of your legs;
for a new turn in the poem of my destiny.

Simply walk through Dublin and you will discover hidden treasures, its buildings, its parks and especially, its people. It's an old city. We know that there were tiny farming and fishing communities living around the centre of present day Dublin five thousand years ago. Over the centuries, the city was shaped by early Christian settlements and invading Vikings and Anglo Normans.

Today, Dublin is a modern and vibrant European capital. Its people are confident and its future is bright.

Dubliners also enjoy many advantages. In the Phoenix Park, we have 1,700 acres of parkland practically in the centre of the city. I know of no other capital city which can boast such a vast amenity. You are also never too far from the coastline. And take a trip of less than 20 miles south and you are in Wicklow - the Garden of Ireland. Less than 30 miles to the north, you can visit the ancient burial tombs of Newgrange. Step onto a boat on the Grand Canal in my native Drumcondra and you can navigate your way to the midlands.

Dublin and Dubliners have so much to offer. I am proud to say it is my home. And my favourite place.

An Taoiseach, Mr. Bertie Ahern T.D

Dublin

The Hills of Connemara

Unknown

Gather up the pots and the old tin cans
The mash, the corn, the barley and the bran.
Run like the devil from the excise man
Keep the smoke from rising, Barney.

Keep your eyes well peeled today
The excise men are on their way
Searching for the mountain tay
In the hills of Connemara.

Swinging to the left, swinging to the right
The excise men will dance all night
Drinkin' up the tay till the broad daylight
In the hills of Connemara

Gather up the pots and the old tin cans
The mash, the corn, the barley and the bran.
Run like the devil from the excise man
Keep the smoke from rising, Barney.

A gallon for the butcher and a quart for John
And a bottle for poor old Father Tom
Just to help the poor old dear along
In the hills of Connemara.

Stand your ground, for it's too late
The excise men are at the gate.
Glory be to Paddy, but they're drinkin' it straight
In the hills of Connemara

Gather up the pots and the old tin cans
The mash, the corn, the barley and the bran.
Run like the devil from the excise man
Keep the smoke from rising, Barney.

Gather up the pots and the old tin cans
The mash, the corn, the barley and the bran.
Run like the devil from the excise man
Keep the smoke from rising, Barney.

Field of Buttercups, Connemara

"Errigal Mountain, Co. Donegal. It's a proper mountain - conical, naked, stately, haunting. It dominates the bleak and painfully beautiful North - West corner of the county. Summer holidays as a child invariably included a climb. From the summit you can see America."

Ardal O'Hanlan - Actor / Comedian

Errigal Mountain

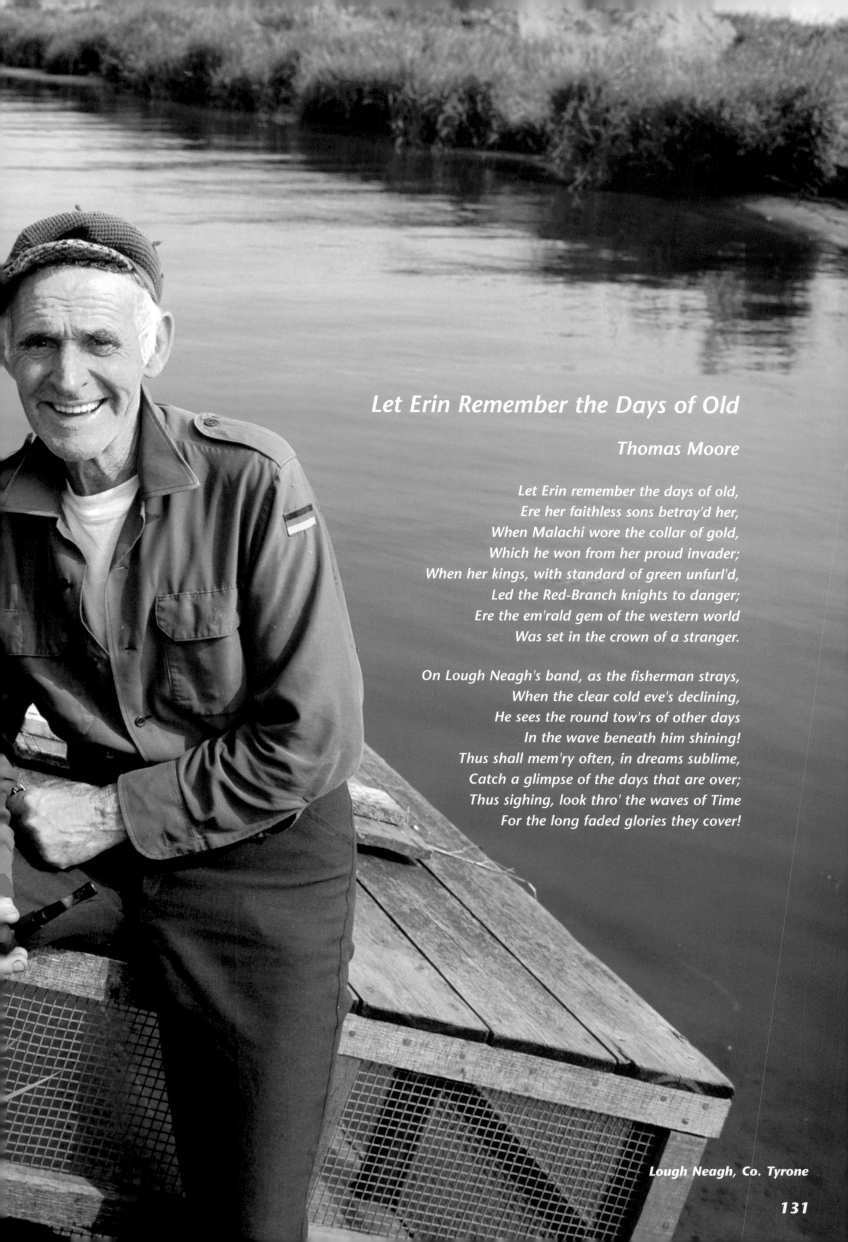

Let Erin Remember the Days of Old

Thomas Moore

Let Erin remember the days of old,
Ere her faithless sons betray'd her,
When Malachi wore the collar of gold,
Which he won from her proud invader;
When her kings, with standard of green unfurl'd,
Led the Red-Branch knights to danger;
Ere the em'rald gem of the western world
Was set in the crown of a stranger.

On Lough Neagh's band, as the fisherman strays,
When the clear cold eve's declining,
He sees the round tow'rs of other days
In the wave beneath him shining!
Thus shall mem'ry often, in dreams sublime,
Catch a glimpse of the days that are over;
Thus sighing, look thro' the waves of Time
For the long faded glories they cover!

Lough Neagh, Co. Tyrone

ARTHY'S Bar

"I would have to choose Castletown Beare on the Beare Peninsula on the south west tip of Cork as my favourite place. I found it seven years ago as I performed my first gig there and stayed for four months. It's a small town but the most amazing place. It's a farming and fishing village where the sunshines loudly and the rain falls beautifully. Of course, my favourite pub in it is McCarthys which appears on the book **McCarthy's Bar** - a book by John Mc Carthy. Basically it's a lovely lovely place with lovely lovely people and I want to buy a house there!"

Colin Farrell - Actor

Castletown Beare

133

Las Vegas in the Hills of Donegal

Pete Gallagher

You may talk about Atlantis, how it's lost beneath the sea
Or the grave of the unknown soldier and the cry of the old banshee
Who was the man in the iron mask, was Jack the ripper set free?
But ask them all where's Donegal, and it's still a mystery

And if I could I'd build a wall around old Donegal
The north and south to keep them out, my god I'd build it tall
Casinoes, chicken ranches, I'd legalize them all
We'd have our own Las Vegas in the hills of Donegal
Yeah!! Las Vegas in the hills of Donegal

Lay by clubs and all night pubs, black jack and roulette
Mel Gibson, Brigitte Nilsen, Mike Tyson having a bet (bite)
Iniseoghain would then be known for its multi-millionaires
Where Donald Trump would have a chunk to live in solitaire

And if I could I'd build a wall around old Donegal
The north and south to keep them out, my god I'd build it tall
Casinoes, chicken ranches, I'd legalize them all
We'd have our own Las Vegas in the hills of Donegal
Yeah!! Las Vegas in the hills of Donegal

To stand on top of fairy hill would give me such a thrill
I've heard them say in Dublin there's gold in them there hills
So don't despair, 'cos if you dare, the answer lies with me
There's a wall that's steep and it's going cheap somewhere in Germany

And if I could I'd build a wall around old Donegal
The north and south to keep them out, my god I'd build it tall
Casinoes, chicken ranches, I'd legalize them all
We'd have our own Las Vegas in the hills of Donegal
Yeah!! Las Vegas in the hills of Donegal

Glengesh, Co. Donegal

Mary Pat tells me that my favourite place in Ireland is the Curracloe Beach in Co. Wexford, where we met 30 years ago on Whit weekend.

Eddie Shaw - Chairman National Safety Council

Curracloe Beach, Co. Wexford

Forty Shades of Green

Johnny Cash

I close my eyes and picture the emerald of the sea
from the fishin boats at Dingle to the shores at Dunehea
I miss the River Shannon and the folks at Skibbereen
the moorlands and meadows and their Forty Shades of Green

But most of all I miss a girl in Tipperary town
and most of all I miss her lips as soft as eiderdown
I long again to see and do the things we've done and seen
where the breeze is sweet as shalimar and there's Forty Shades of Green

I wish that I could spend an hour at Dublin's churning suft
I long to watch the farmers drain the bogs and spade the turf
to see again the thatching of the straw the women clean
I'd walk from Cork to Larne to see those Forty Shades of Green

But most of all I miss a girl in Tipperary town
and most of all I miss her lips as soft as eiderdown
I long again to see and do the things we've done and seen
where the breeze is sweet as shalimar and there's Forty Shades of Green

Shannon Erne Waterway

139

This silent little island has fascinated me since childhood. Its contemporary tranquility belies a surprising dramatic past. It holds the graves of the tragic Úna Bhán and her forbidden lover Tomas Costelloe.

The Priory, long since in ruins was a place as much of ecclesiastical intrigue as high scholarship. Home of the famous manuscript The Annals of Lough Cé, Ireland's turbulent history creates an unnervingly edgy mood here- a place of memory rather than meditation.

Close to my father's home the Forrest Park is a place I return to again and again, grateful to belong to the first generation privileged to have the gift of easy public access to this magnificent landscape.

Mary Mc Aleese - President of Ireland

Trinity Island, Lough Key Forrest Park, Boyle, Co. Roscommon

The Mountains of Mourne

Percy French

Oh Mary, this London's a wonderful sight,
With people here working by day and by night.
They don't sow potatoes nor barley nor wheat
But there's gangs of them diggin' for gold in the street.
At least, when I asked them that's what I was told
So I just took a hand at this diggin' for gold;
But for all that I've found there, I might as well be
Where the Mountains of Mourne sweep down to the sea.

Mourne Mountains

On the comparatively bare, rocky peninsula of Beara - contrasting greatly with Dingle above it - lies a small strip of coastline facing westward up the broad expanse of the Kenmare Estuary and out into the Atlantic.

Here, on a fine day, you can discern the hills and distant headlands of Dingle, beyond which rears the enormous vertical hump of Scariff Island, on which people still lived energetically up to some 50 years ago. All about you lies the presence of the sea with its unpredictable mood, overhung by the widest sky imaginable, constantly on the move.

My wife, Anne Madden, sees this unique place, as "the most dramatic meeting of land, sea and sky on earth." I agree!

Louis le Brocquy - Artist

Beara From Sheep's Head, Co.Cork

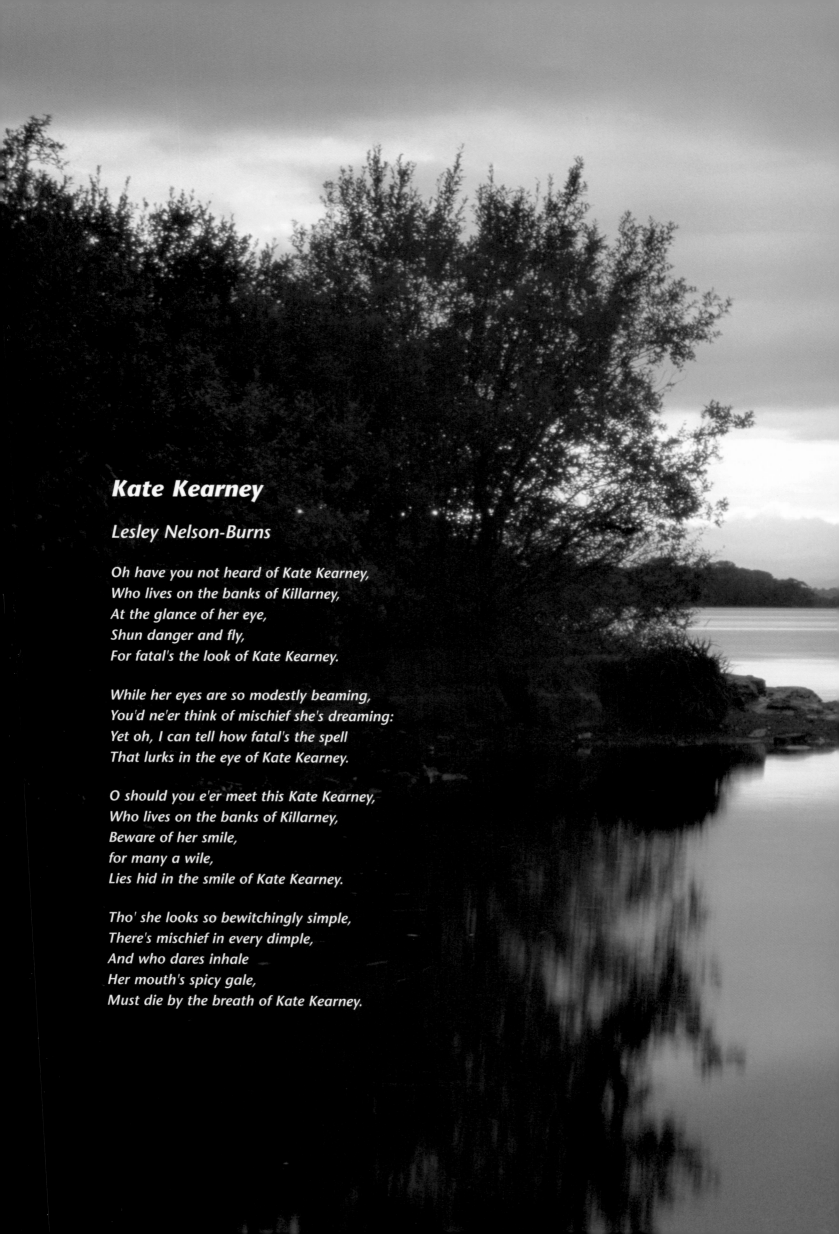

Kate Kearney

Lesley Nelson-Burns

Oh have you not heard of Kate Kearney,
Who lives on the banks of Killarney,
At the glance of her eye,
Shun danger and fly,
For fatal's the look of Kate Kearney.

While her eyes are so modestly beaming,
You'd ne'er think of mischief she's dreaming:
Yet oh, I can tell how fatal's the spell
That lurks in the eye of Kate Kearney.

O should you e'er meet this Kate Kearney,
Who lives on the banks of Killarney,
Beware of her smile,
for many a wile,
Lies hid in the smile of Kate Kearney.

Tho' she looks so bewitchingly simple,
There's mischief in every dimple,
And who dares inhale
Her mouth's spicy gale,
Must die by the breath of Kate Kearney.

Lowerlake

Picking a favourite place in Ireland is not easy - there's Clare and The Burren; there's Kerry and the Dingle Penninsula; there's Mayo. I could go on and on.
I've plumped for Dublin. Born in Glasnevin, on the Northside, the cultured side! I was educated in the city when Scoil Chaitriona was in Eccles Street. I have lived outside Dublin for decades but I just love going back in.

I love the people, I love the Green and the Park. I love the streets, the river, the canals, and the accents.

I complain about it, rail about the traffic, despair about some developments - but it's like the proverbial well worn shoes.

I've friends there, memories there and even as it changed, it's comfortable and it's mine.

Marion Finucane - Broadcaster

Financial Centre, Dublin

149

Digging

Seamus Heaney

Between my finger and my thumb
The squat pen rests; snug as a gun.

Under my window, a clean rasping sound
When the spade sinks into gravelly ground:
My father, digging. I look down

Till his straining rump among the flowerbeds
Bends low, comes up twenty years away
Stooping in rhythm through potato drills
Where he was digging.

The coarse boot nestled on the lug, the shaft
Against the inside knee was levered firmly.
He rooted out tall tops, buried the bright edge deep
To scatter new potatoes that we picked
Loving their cool hardness in our hands.

By God, the old man could handle a spade.
Just like his old man.

My grandfather cut more turf in a day
Than any other man on Toner's bog.
Once I carried him milk in a bottle
Corked sloppily with paper. He straightened up
To drink it, then fell to right away

Nicking and slicing neatly, heaving sods
Over his shoulder, going down and down
For the good turf. Digging.

The cold smell of potato mould, the squelch and slap
Of soggy peat, the curt cuts of an edge
Through living roots awaken in my head.
But I've no spade to follow men like them.

Between my finger and my thumb
The squat pen rests
I'll dig with it.

Dingle, Co Kerry

The Hills of Kerry

Unknown

The palm trees wave on high along the fertile shore
Adieu the Hills of Kerry I ne'er will see no more.
Oh why did I leave my home, oh why did I cross the sea.
And leave the small birds singing around you sweet Tralee?

The noble and the brave have departed from our shore
They've gone, the've gone to fight the war where wild, the canons roar.
No more they'll see the shamrock, the plant so dear to me,
Or hear the small birds singing around you sweet Tralee.

No more the sun will shine on that blessed harvest morn
Or hear our reaper singing in a golden field of corn
There's a balm for every woe and a cure for every pain,
But the smiling face of my darling girl I will never see again.

Ring Of Kerry

Parting Glass

Traditional

Of all the money that e'er I spent
I've spent it in good company
And all the harm that ever I did
Alas it was to none but me
And all I've done for want of wit
To memory now I can't recall
So fill to me the parting glass
Good night and joy be with you all

If I had money enough to spend
And leisure to sit awhile
There is a fair maid in the town
That sorely has my heart beguiled
Her rosy cheeks and ruby lips
I own she has my heart enthralled
So fill to me the parting glass
Good night and joy be with you all

Oh, all the comrades that e'er I had
They're sorry for my going away
And all the sweethearts that e'er I had
They'd wish me one more day to stay
But since it falls unto my lot
That I should rise and you should not
I'll gently rise and softly call
Good night and joy be with you all

Madden's Bar, Belfast

155

I admire many parts of Rural Ireland but essentially I am an urbanist who loves cities and the dynamic of urban living. Dublin is my favourite part of Ireland with its social and civic institutions. Restaurant Patrick Guilband is one of my favourite places in Dublin. To my mind it continues the great traditions of Dublin hostelries such as Jammets, the Russell and the Lafayette where generations of Dubliners dined with grace and elegance.

Arthur Gibney - President Royal Hibernian Academy of Arts

156

Tourism is an Irish success story.

Tourism delivers €5 billion in revenue

Tourism is doing a vital economic job for Ireland. With €4 billion spent by visitors to Ireland and almost €1 billion spent on domestic trips in 2003, tourism contributed an estimated €2.3 billion to the Exchequer, and accounts for 4.4% of GNP. An estimated 230,000 people are employed in the Irish tourism and catering industry.

Failte Ireland is the national tourism development authority dedicated to Irish tourism. It provides strategic and practical support to develop and sustain Ireland as a high quality and competitive tourist destination. Established by Government, Fáilte Ireland works in partnership with the tourism industry.

As the first tourism industry 'one stop shop', Fáilte Ireland delivers services across Industry Development, Education & Training and Market Development.

Fáilte Ireland

www.failteireland.ie
Tel: 1890 525 525
info@failteireland.ie